SWAYAMBHU

conversations with death

SWAYAMBHU

conversations with death

Eric-Jan Verwey

BOOKS

Winchester, UK
Washington, USA

First published by O-Books, 2013
O-Books is an imprint of John Hunt Publishing Ltd., Laurel House, Station Approach,
Alresford, Hants, SO24 9JH, UK
office1@jhpbooks.net
www.johnhuntpublishing.com

For distributor details and how to order please visit the 'Ordering' section on our website.

Text copyright: Eric-Jan Verwey 2012

ISBN: 978 1 78099 443 7

A CIP catalogue record for this book is available from the British Library.

Printed and bound by CPI Group (UK) Ltd, Croydon, CR0 4YY

We operate a distinctive and ethical publishing philosophy in all
areas of our business, from our global network of authors to
production and worldwide distribution.

About the author

Eric-Jan Verwey was fascinated by and drawn to religious mysticism from a very early age. As soon as he was old enough to travel alone, he went to India and, experiencing the power of the temples and myths of this ancient culture, has been making pilgrimages there ever since. Through a strange set of circumstances and an illness, his path eventually led him to Israel where a compassionate rabbi helped him and started him on his path towards linguistic Kabbalah. Returning to his homeland, Eric was inspired to master the Hebrew language in order to gain access to the source texts of this stream of mysticism. He completed a masters degree in Semitic languages and spent a year studying at the University of Jerusalem. Now he combines daily study of medieval kabbalistic texts with regular trips to India visiting ever-more obscure and ancient Hindu temples. In between he also explores other streams of mysticism such as Zen Buddhism and Tibetan Buddhism. Eric has turned to writing as a way of deepening his own mystical experiences and his novels are an outcome of this. His writing process is not a conventional one, and he uses a free-flowing technique where he is unaware of the outcome and follows signs and intuitions as they arise while he writes. He intersperses his writing with his studies and is constantly surprised and delighted by the revelations this combination yields. His books can be read as fictional novels but more than that they are the stream of conciousness and real-time experiences of a contemporary mystic.

WWW.TOKAILASHANDBEYOND.COM

to Pinnih

CONTENTS

Swayambhu; conversations with death is the third part of the trilogy *Swayambhu,* the first two parts of which are *To Kailash and Beyond* and *The Absence of Direction.* As a result, many of the kabbalistic ideas that *Swayambhu; conversations with death* freely elaborates on will be found in these two novels as well. In *The Absence of Direction,* having already done so in *To Kailash and Beyond,* I chose to use these ideas without explaining their workings in a very detailed manner. In order not to inconvenience the reader who has not read *To Kailash and Beyond* or *The Absence of Direction,* but who wants to familiarize themselves with the remarks on Jewish mysticism as made in *To Kailash and Beyond,* I have also included a brief explanation in the introduction to this novel.

Swayambhu differs from the first two parts of the trilogy in two main ways. The first way is how the rudimentary kabbalistic ideas used are introduced and explained. In *To Kailash and Beyond* I felt I needed to outline them in some detail, which I did in the introduction. In *The Absence of Direction* I relied upon those explanations, referring the reader to them, and only reiterating the basics in the introduction. In *Swayambhu; conversations with death* I have repeated this course of action, but have approached the inclusion of explanation in the narration differently. In the main body of the text one will find hardly any references to kabbalistic terminology, and no explicit explanation. At the end, though, I have added an endnote apparatus, revealing in a running detailed commentary most if not all of the hidden references of part 1.

The second way in which *Swayambhu* differs from the first two volumes of the trilogy is in how the sentences on which those two volumes are built, are derived. Although the central topic of all three novels is mystical death, in *Swayambhu; conversations with death* death is not present as the extraction of every ninth letter from the first book of the Hebrew Bible (for the reasoning behind this exercise, see the appendix part 3 of *The Absence of Direction: Behind the scenes*) as is the case in the first two volumes. In *Swayambhu; conversations with death* I have instead projected the word for death, *mavet*, מות, directly onto the text of the first book of the Hebrew Bible. I have done this by taking the numerical values of the letters that make up this word for death (the value 40 of its first letter *mem*, the value six of its second letter *vav*, and the value 400 of its last letter *tav*), and choosing the letters from Genesis accordingly. Hence the first letter of those that form the foundation of this novel is the 40th letter of Genesis; the second letter is the 6th after that 40th, the 46th letter of Genesis; and the third the 400th after that 46th letter, the 446th letter of Genesis. Having thus projected the word for death onto the book of Genesis once, I started over, again taking the 40th letter after the last one extracted, etc. I have done so five times. Since the word for death has three letters, projecting them onto the text five times gave me fifteen letters. In the endnotes to this novel these fifteen letters are referred to as 'the fifteen foundation letters of the novel'.

The significance of fifteen is made clear in the endnotes to the novel itself.

The fifteen letters gathered in this way, with the total numerical value of 682, are the *vav, chet, bet, heh, yud, bet, ayin, peh, lamed, aleph, bet, khaf, tav, vav*, and *mem*: מ ו-ח-ב-ה-י-ב-ע-פ-ל-א-ב-כ-ת-ו.

INTRODUCTION

Of central importance to understanding Jewish letter mysticism in general is the fact that every letter in the Hebrew alphabet has a number assigned to it. The practice of converting words and sentences into numbers, after which they can be compared with other words of the same numerical value, and similarities drawn, is known as *gematriah*: the numerology of the Hebrew language and alphabet. In addition to the use of *gematriah* various other systems are used including those that recognise a correlation between the ten *sefirot*, or emanations and manifestations of the Godhead, and the twenty-two letters in the Hebrew alphabet. Words that have the same numerical value thus not only share the same qualities, but also reveal more aspects of the Divine.

Combining all these factors, one gets an outline like the one in table 1.

To illustrate how the outline given above can help us understand numerology and find connections between numbers and the *sefirot*, I would like to summon the reader's attention to the word אדם, or *adam*, meaning man.

Looking up the three letters *aleph*, *dalet* and *mem* (reading from right to left as is the case in Hebrew) comprising the word *adam* in the columns headed **glyph** or **Hebrew** we find the numerical values of these letters in the column headed **number** to the left of them. The numerical value of the word *adam* (45) equals the sum total of the numbers connected to those letters (1, 4, and 40).

Table 1

NUMBER	HEBREW	GLYPH	TEN SEFIROT	GODLY NAMES
1	*Aleph*	א	*Keter* - Crown	*Ehuyeh Asher Ehuyeh*
2	*Bet*	ב	*Chokhmah* - Wisdom	*Yah*
3	*Gimmel*	ג	*Binah* - Understanding	*YHVH (read Elohim)*
4	*Dalet*	ד	*Chesed* - Love	*El*
5	*Heh*	ה	*Din/Geburah* - Judgment/Strength	*Elohim*
6	*Vav*	ו	*Tiferet* - Beauty	*YHVH (read Adonai)*
7	*Zayin*	ז	*Netsach* - Victory	*Adonai Tsevaot*
8	*Chet*	ח	*Hod* - Grace	*Elohim Tsevaot*
9	*Tet*	ט	*Yesod* - Foundation	*Shadai (El Chai)*
10	*Yud*	י	*Malkhut* - Kingdom	*Adonai*
20	*Khaf*	כ		
30	*Lamed*	ל		
40	*Mem*	מ		
50	*Nun*	נ		
60	*Samekh*	ס		
70	*Ayin*	ע		
80	*Peh*	פ		
90	*Tsadi*	צ		
100	*Kuf*	ק		
200	*Resh*	ר		
300	*Shin*	ש		
400	*Tav*	ת		

The only thing complicating this example is the fact that the last letter of the word *adam* is the final form the *mem* takes, which, for simplifying reasons, is not included in the outline.

To continue with the example, the word *adam* can be connected to the second *sefirah* called *Chokhmah*, חכמה, in the following way. The last part of this word, *mah*, מה, comprising the letters *mem* and *heh* with the values 40 and 5, has the same numerical value as *adam*, 45. Taking *mah* away from the complete word *Chokhmah*, what is left is *chokh*, חכ. Reversing the two Hebrew letters, this is pronounced *koach*, כח, and means strength or potential.

When we then combine the meaning of this first part of *Chokhmah*, and that of *adam*, sharing its numerological value with the second part of *Chokhmah*, we reach the end of this modest example. *Chokhmah*, literally meaning wisdom, now also reveals itself as the strength or potential of man.

Another topic often encountered in Jewish letter mysticism is that of permutations. There are many different systems of permutation; some so common that they are even accepted by people having nothing to do with mysticism, and yet others that are very esoteric. What they all have in common is that they offer ways in which the letters of the Hebrew alphabet can be interchanged, permuted.

Typically in a permutation system, the letters of the Hebrew alphabet are organised in two rows, each row containing all 22 letters. In one row, the source row, the letters appear in their normal sequence, running from the first letter *aleph* to the last letter *tav*. In the second row, the sequence of letters, while still following the traditional sequence, is reversed. The corresponding letters from each row form pairs of letters that can be interchanged and whose outcomes are taken as a deeper meaning of the original word.

One of the most common systems of permutation is called *atbash* (see table 2). It interchanges the first letter of the Hebrew alphabet, the *aleph*,

Table 2: The atbash method

NAME OF LETTER IN NORMAL SEQUENCE	NORMAL SEQUENCE OF ALPHABET	NUMBER ASSIGNED TO LETTER	*ATBASH* SEQUENCE	NUMBER OF *ATBASH*
Aleph	א	1	ת	400
Bet	ב	2	ש	300
Gimmel	ג	3	ר	200
Dalet	ד	4	ק	100
Heh	ה	5	צ	90
Vav	ו	6	פ	80
Zayin	ז	7	ע	70
Chet	ח	8	ס	60
Tet	ט	9	נ	50
Yud	י	10	מ	40
Khaf	כ	20	ל	30
Lamed	ל	30	כ	20
Mem	מ	40	י	10
Nun	נ	50	ט	9
Samekh	ס	60	ח	8
Ayin	ע	70	ז	7
Peh	פ	80	ו	6
Tsadi	צ	90	ה	5
Kuf	ק	100	ד	4
Resh	ר	200	ג	3
Shin	ש	300	ב	2
Tav	ת	400	א	1

with the last, the *tav*, and the second, the *bet*, with the penultimate, the *shin*, and so on. Hence the name of the method: the 'a' becomes the 't', the 'b' the 'sh': *atbash*.

When using systems like *atbash*, a mystic may in some cases permute a whole word or sentence, and in others only the so-called root letters of a word. The term root letters refers to the three letters that form the base of every word in Hebrew. Conjugating these root letters forms nouns, verbs, adjectives, etc.

I would like to use the first word of the Hebrew Bible as an example of how to use the *atbash* system. This word for 'in the beginning' is *bereshit*, בראשית. (Remember to read the Hebrew from right to left.)

To calculate the normal numerology of this word, we copy the actions performed when calculating the value of the word *adam*. That is, take the word chosen, בראשית, and look up the numbers next to each of the letters (ב, *bet*; ר, *resh*; א, *aleph*; ש, *shin*; י, *yud*; and ת, *tav*) in the column headed **number assigned to letter**. You will find that they add up to 913.

If you wish to calculate the *atbash* value of this word, then look at the column headed **atbash sequence**, and interchange the letters of the original word with the letters they are paired with in the *atbash* column. After this, look up the numbers of the *atbash* equivalents as found in the column to the right of them, **number of atbash**, and add them together.

You will find that the *atbash* of 'in the beginning', *bereshit*, 913, is שגתבמא, *shin*, *gimmel*, *tav*, *bet*, *mem*, and *aleph*, bearing the numbers 1-40-2-400-3-300. The sum total of the *atbash* value of 'in the beginning' is therefore 746.

The references in this book are quoted as per the Hebrew Bible: Biblia Hebraica Stuttgartensia (Stuttgart 1997). Where there are differences with English versions, these will be given in brackets after those as per the Hebrew Bible.

Swayambhu

CHAPTER I

THE SECRET SOUL GARDEN

In temporal creation there are no immediate counterparts to the highest three sefirot; here, love and severity are not distinguished or separated from each other.

They had left via the crumbled section of the western fortifications. Only when they reached the town sacred to the Gathering of the Nine[1] and started making their way to the adjacent lake sacred to the Gathering of the Five,[2] did they get their first glimpse of the walls. It made them realize that, unbeknownst to them, there had always been a plan.

They made their way through the ruins vigilantly, taking heed not to climb any of the mountains of rubble lying about, nor touch their borders (Ex. 19:12),[3] and reached the lake's shores without drawing any blood.[4] They instantly knew he was watching them. Turning their backs to him without any hostile or even disrespectful motions, things turned with them. This much they had expected. Even amongst the nomadic warlocks it was widely known that wherever the five ascertained itself directly, nothing stayed the same for very long. The five was simply too fond of change. While things submitted to the pull of transformation, he moved as well, but with everything shifting at the same time, it was impossible for them to notice this.

Change hovered over the lake for a while, blowing life[5] into now the seals, and then their amorphous recipients. As a result, the waters divided

(Gen. 1:6) and the ones susceptible to life were impregnated by aspects of time.[6] Behold the secrets, brace yourselves for the exquisiteness of what is within your reach.

Ripples began to swirl over the lake, anticipating the formless existence it felt stirring inside. As they watched, a living soul[7] permeated the lake, spreading through it like a liquid groom in search of a prospective bride, following up on heaven's desire to form a name.[8] For a moment abundance's impatience projected the wildest creatures imaginable. But, understanding that only through the mediation of the full name would falsehood and truth[9] both have their designated places, it accepted the mould and coins appeared on the bottom of the lake, close to shore. First she, and then he, waded through the shallow waters to pick them up. Together they managed to collect fifteen[10] of them, more they could not see, and less they dared not elevate.

'Not exactly small change,' their observer chuckled. 'Will they see them as half or as full, I wonder.'[11]

His words travelled equally in distance, intensity, and timbre in all directions. They entered his makeshift shelter under the shady Oochira trees, increasing the freshness inside, tantalizing the air. They enjoyed tracing the walls flanking one side of the lake, playing with the dancing reflection of the small waves that the sun cast on them. They bestrode the lake's surface and toyed with the figures standing knee-deep in the water, swirling around them like the coiling starry trace left by a magic wand, before finally allowing themselves to be heard. He who heard first did so on a subconscious level and formed the phrase as if it were his own.

'Would you say fifteen is half or all?' No-one Going Nowhere asked.

'I would say that each thing that comprises an earlier phase of another thing can be said to contain that later phase fully,' Tamar answered.

'That makes sense,' No-one Going Nowhere said. 'So let's stay with the number we are holding in our hands,' he added, practically.

They continued walking away from the shore, towards the lake's centre, he holding ten coins, and she five. Just before the water became too deep, they diverted to a small island and there constructed a make-shift raft and some paddles for navigation. Just in case, they spent half an hour stocking up on provisions, consisting mostly of fruits and nuts. Then they pushed their raft off in the hope of making it to the clear waters of the ocean. They only needed to paddle for fifteen twinklings of the eye before a friendly current got hold of them. From then onwards, there were no more obligations and they were free to do whatever they wished. Limited in their options by their lack of possessions, they returned their attention to the fifteen coins spread out on the bottom of their boat.

'The white owl once told me that this world was created by means of the letter *heh*, the five, and the world to come by means of the letter *yud*, the ten,'[12] No-one Going Nowhere pondered. 'Do you think that tells us something about those worlds' comparative qualities?'

'Possibly,' Tamar answered, 'but it certainly tells us that our souls, as part of those worlds, were imprinted with two inclinations.'[13]

'A pull towards the truth and a pull towards untruth,' No-one Going Nowhere agreed.

'But in the fullness of the outstanding name[14] those two are absolved, which in practise is brought about by actuating the living soul,'[15] Tamar posed.

No-one Going Nowhere knew she was right, and readied himself for the renewal of the twenty-two's fifteen representatives[16] that they had prepared for their voyage.

As if waiting for this, the coins' heads swallowed their tails, leaving fifteen black holes in the bottom of the boat. Not having expected the coins to act this ruthlessly, and quite uncomfortable with the sudden precarious state of their raft, the young warlocks quickly recited their list of fifteen letters. To their relief, this unprecedented, and prodigiously self-affirming, gathering[17] proved fitting. The letters filled the holes that the coins had left and, the danger of sinking averted, No-one Going Nowhere and Tamar settled into embellishing each letter with fifteen different vowels. Again abundance readied itself, but they knew the simple cure for this to be the mention of the god of death's name.[18]

With their raft now contained, charged, and electrified, this male and female breathed more easily.[19] Confrontation[20] had commenced and the warlocks were charmed.

It came to pass after these things that No-one Going Nowhere confused their fate for a postponement,[21] and he became restless. His sickness was so sore (1 Kings 17:17)[22] that soon there was no breath left in him. Seeing his condition for what it was, this did not upset Tamar. With a cupped hand she scooped up some water and measured it. In her mind she calculated the dust of the earth (Isaiah 40:12), and weighed the mountains of their native village on scales. She then apportioned the hills through which they had walked during the first days of their journey to the western fortifications, and found the balance she was after.[23] No longer out of breath, No-one Going Nowhere was left filled with love,[24] and many other things pertaining to half the name.[25]

'From the fullness of the half[26] to the Sacred Number[27] in a matter of minutes: these youngsters surely know how to actuate the soul[28] of things,' their observer commented admiringly. 'This will give them some breathing space, I imagine.'

It did. For days after the two warlocks had partaken of the written word and skilfully used of the number fifteen in order to excavate the numerical signature from its splendid necropolis,[29] the script did not cross their paths in a literal way. They spent most of their time telling each other stories from the days when myths and reality never contradicted one another, could not contradict one another, since the mind had not yet succumbed to matter. Tamar exhibited a special affection for the chronicles of the living sanctuaries,[30] narrating the adventures with a personal passion and feminine flair that No-one Going Nowhere had never encountered in her before. No-one Going Nowhere again discovered within himself a predilection for treading tracks through the wild, using descriptions to lead him to forms, forms to tell him about numbers, and numbers to guide him to Meaninglessness. In general Tamar relished these linguistic acrobatics immensely, but when they tied in with her own genealogy in particular, she simply lost herself in the void and formlessness that constituted her soul.[31]

At one point, when No-one Going Nowhere reminded Tamar of the name denoting her true spouse, and of their combined worth,[32] she could not help adding to this, unobtrusively reminding No-one Going Nowhere of the tents of wisdom.[33] This reminder brought tears of joy to No-one Going Nowhere's eyes and fanned the fire of his zeal. From then onwards the young warlocks were locked in a gracious non-competitive engagement, replacing names by names,[34] actuating all over again. Of course this drew down the creative energies behind the work of the chariot,[35] which could only have one effect.

No-one Going Nowhere and Tamar interrupted their battle[36] to watch their raft change its course and head for the river Khebar.[37] They moored at the fourth branch of this river[38] and disembarked.

A secret garden[39] was awaiting them. It was hidden from their view by wild growth; massive thorny shrubs that to Tamar looked like brambles without fruit. Whatever the prickly fiends were, their defence weapons would keep out anyone not determined to accomplish the opposite, and even then only if equipped with some sharp and sturdy tools. Not having any reason to be thus determined, the two warlocks made their way along the hedge, assuming they were on some sort of path. They walked along the auspicious river[40] for some distance before turning left away from the river bank. After about an hour's walk and two more sharp turns to the left, they found themselves back at the river Khebar. Seeing their moored boat, they understood they had in fact been mistaking something's perimeter for a trail. This prompted their curiosity. Discussing what the natural fence might be sheltering, No-one Going Nowhere proposed that its four corners might give them some clue. Asked by Tamar to explain, he pointed out that those corners had looked unusual or, rather, felt unusual to him. Didn't she remember that they had both hesitated as to which direction to follow at each corner they had encountered, even though each time there had only been one path ahead of them?

'It is almost as if the corners themselves offer some kind of alternative passage...,' No-one Going Nowhere mused.

'The existence of another, hidden, way would definitely account for the indecisiveness we felt,' Tamar agreed.

They decided to walk the rectangular route once more, and to this time pay more attention to the mysterious energy of its corners. Somehow it didn't occur to them to start their investigation with the corner they had just turned, and instead they proceeded to the next one, a short walk along the Khebar.

'If you had to give each of the four corners a colour,' Tamar suggested a game they had often played when they were young, 'what would they be?'

No-one Going Nowhere was aware that Tamar was more interested in the numbers than in the colours he would come up with. Since she knew precisely which number, according to him, belonged to which colour, this was her unobtrusive way of finding them out all the same. No-one Going Nowhere played along.

'All four of them are aerial colours,' he began, but then realised how unintelligible that must sound.

'It is as if, trying to grasp the colours of this Hiding Place's[41] four corners,' he started over, expressing the unprecedented difficulty he was faced with in attempting to identify the colours, 'I am seeking that which is lost' (Ezek. 34:16). It feels as if I am attempting to restore[42] that which was driven away,[43] to bind that which was broken. And I am not sure whether that is the right thing to do.'[44]

6

Tamar stopped short and looked at No-one Going Nowhere inquisitively. For his twenty-one years he looked wise, but then again, he always had. And although his bone structure wasn't exceptionally big and his slender limbs not overtly muscular, he was the picture of strength. The power that she saw, she knew, stemmed from both a firm conviction, again firmer than one would expect in someone of his age, and from the experience of seeing his true potential actualised. Whether the experience had preceded the conviction, or whether the conviction had enabled the experiences to take place, she did not know. Perhaps the two were but two sides of the same coin.

At this moment, No-one Going Nowhere looked a little tired, but far from exhausted, and the light of truth shone steady and calm from his eyes.

'I don't know if you realise, but you've just boarded the chariot again,'[45] she said softly, 'and whatever vision comes to you from there need not be questioned. I understand that the prospect of binding that which is unbound deters you, but all depends on the nature of what you are about to bind and what you are binding it to.'[46]

No-one Going Nowhere listened to her carefully and realized once again that although he was the one most versed in matters of the Book, Tamar was far from unschooled herself.

'You are right, it is in the nature of all things to be bound to Nothingness,[47] especially,' and here he thought of the coins they had collected in the lake sacred to the Gathering of the Five, 'when the star of the fifteen is shining bright.[48] But it is colours we are after, and they are far from nothing…'

'How can anything be far from Nothing, when all was created from it,'[49] Tamar said.

No-one Going Nowhere, taking Tamar's point, made another effort to bring her the colours. This time he took extra care to not unintentionally force his way directly to them, but to first follow the pull towards Nothingness, the corners' looseness, and then observe their restoration.

To give it his best shot, No-one Going Nowhere stood as still as a tree on a windless day. He got sucked in and was no longer. This took some time. Then, with a content rustle, he breathed out through all of his leaves and spoke.

'I think the corners' nature does lean towards being bound, but in an unbound kind of way. It seems they somehow accept discernible matter, but that this matter is only held onto fleetingly. They pulsate, like a heart.[50] At moments there most certainly are four colours, four numbers, but then they return and cannot be distinguished from each other.[51] When they reappear, they still contain traces of the original numbers, but are really clothed in others. In short: there is more than one group of four. They bind, but show various layers of binding at the same time. That's why it was so hard to pinpoint them.'

They had started walking again, and were close to the point where they had initially disembarked from their raft.

'Do you know why some call the letter *aleph* an ark?' No-one Going Nowhere digressed involuntarily.[52]

'Because,' he continued, answering his own question, 'the *tav*, the last letter of the alphabet, amounts to 416. Proceeding one more step back to the beginning, swallowing our own tail, we reach the first letter, the *aleph*. This one step brings the 416 up to the 417 of the word for ark, *teivah*. Just to say that all is circular and endless.'

Tamar smiled and nudged him softly with her elbow.

'Right,' he responded with a playful note of guilt. 'Just got carried away by the sight of our trustworthy boat.'

They halted at the corner where the path led away from the river Khebar. Again both of them were instantly overcome with indecisiveness as to the continuation of their walk. This time, however, they were fully aware of it.

'Yes, the four corners' first layer is clearly aerial,' No-one Going Nowhere reiterated. 'What I am sure of, though, is that the corner in front of us harbours a doorway. A doorway, even, to many other doorways. But you asked for a colour, didn't you?'

Tamar was standing behind him, so as not to disturb 'his reading', as she called it, and put her hand on his shoulder affirmatively.

'Well, I am sorry to disappoint you,' No-one Going Nowhere said after a moment or two, 'but the colour of this corner is simply too elusive, too vague, to be captured by words. Its name I can give you, though!'

Not needing an answer to know what Tamar's response would be, No-one Going Nowhere continued. 'For now, I would name this corner the *aleph*, and the other three, who, by the way, are only slightly less intangible, I ascribe the names *heh*, *vav*, and *yud*.'[53]

'That is a very powerful collection of letters,' Tamar whispered. 'Together they are 22 and are the ingredients of both the Tetragrammaton, *yud heh vav heh*, and the name belonging to the Crown.'[54]

'Yes, and I can somehow see those two names flashing up, but not as part of the pulsating layers,' No-one Going Nowhere whispered back, entranced.

His words had a contagious quality that widened his experience, incorporating Tamar. As one, the two warlocks looked at the four letters that No-one Going Nowhere had named, and watched as the two grand names that could be formed by them swung in a circular orbit around an invisible axis, their letters at a fixed distance from each other. Each time one of the names' four letters converged with the four corners, it tried to set them in motion. It wasn't long before they succeeded. The four corners joined the orbit; from the moment of their motion no longer merging with either of the two names' letters, but keeping a set position. No-one Going Nowhere and Tamar observed how the twelve-angulated star revolved faster and faster, and then expanded. When it felt as if the circular force entered their craniums' crowns like the arm of a wild sweeping cyclone, they had a flash of the letters as cosmic constellations, and then were inside the enclosure. Inside the secret soul garden.

The first thing they both noticed was that from the inside they could not detect the thorny hedge that, from outside, had blocked their way in. The second thing they learnt was that the environment inside wasn't as immobile as environments usually tend to be.

Where the hedge logically should have been, the rolling meadows and mountains that made up the centre of this Hiding Place continued unperturbed. Well, almost unperturbed. Where the garden should have ended faint shapes hung stationary in the air, at about the same height as the top of the formerly formidable hedge. These shapes hung as if suspended by threads, which, if they really were there, were as invisible as the hedge. Once No-one Going Nowhere had ascertained that Tamar was seeing the same shapes as he thought he was seeing, he walked up to them and tried to touch them. Although his fingers went straight through them, a soft, but still clearly audible sound was heard at the moment he had expected to feel something. Like the sound a crystal glass makes when it is tapped with a spoon. As if waiting on this resonance to give them the go-ahead, upon its ringing all the vacuous figures retreated and four large, distinct shapes appeared, immediately identified by No-one Going Nowhere and Tamar as letters. They positioned themselves around the warlocks, forming the four corners of a square, but No-one Going Nowhere and Tamar did not have to look around at them to know which letters they were. It could not have been different. It was all according to the plan that they had first become aware of when coming upon the walls. The four letters were the same as the first four they had prepared for their journey: the *vav*, the *chet*, the *bet*, and the *heh*.

'I am,' No-one Going Nowhere opened.

'Who I am,' Tamar completed.

Or, at least, that's what she had intended to do. It would have been proper, seeing that the four letters amounted to 21, just as the first part of the name belonging to the highest *sefirah* did: *Ehuyeh*, אהיה. But she didn't get as far as saying the three words that were on the tip of her tongue. Instead, she got as far as saying, 'Who'. Maybe because she thought she felt a hand resting on her shoulder after pronouncing that word, a princely hand filling her with so much peace that all intentions of saying more were simply forgotten.[55] But more likely it was because there seemed to be something crucial to their journey stirring within her when she pronounced that word. And that something took up all her attention, leaving her, if not disinterested in, then certainly too preoccupied for, the remainder of the lofty name.

'"Who", *asher*, 501, אשר,' No-one Going Nowhere repeated, now resigning himself to the fact that Tamar was at least as versed in matters of the Book as he was.

The both of them were taken up by this word, cognising but not knowing its secrets. They lost interest in the four letters stoically reclining in the wild grass, and began strolling over the land. Further down the slope, partly concealed by a dip in the field, they saw the back of a running gazelle[56] popping up with playful regularity. The presence of the beautiful animal excited them and they hurried through the tall grasses towards it, careful not to trample on the lilies that were growing where the thorns had been.[57]

Arriving at the top of the hollow that had partly hidden the gazelle from sight, a new image[58] was awaiting them. With the friendliness of a tree the image begged them to come closer,[59] but, while they navigated the surprisingly large white boulders scattered about like so many giant mushrooms, the image fled away like a shadow (Song of Solomon 2:17). Like *his* shadow, they both thought, without knowing why.[60] The fugitive image was far from shy. At moments during their pursuit of it, just when they turned the corner of a mountain path, or stepped out from a forest into an open field, it would be almost within touching distance. At those moments, though, it no longer reminded them of a tree. Unless it was the kind of tree that had a furnace for a trunk and rays for branches. Five times the image sprang on them like a raging light. Five times, and then it no longer fled from them, then it filled their hearts.[61]

CHAPTER 2

—— ✿ ——

THE GATE OF YOUR DEATH

The appearance of stillness resulting from two equal and opposite forces underlies the symbolism of the mathematical zero.

The image first filled all of their heart and then all of their soul.[62] Then it began filling something else, but even though it satiated them, they couldn't say exactly what it was. They agreed that whatever it was, it couldn't contain all that was poured into it. Sure enough, it overflowed, and handed them precisely one extra measurement.[63] Taking into account that they had no idea what was going on, they accepted it quite gracefully. Then, with the same outward posture of containment, they stored the extra measurement.

'For when the blood will come.' The thought hit them both at the same time, without the interference of understanding.

The blood came almost immediately.

'What is this?' Tamar cried out, just before it engulfed her.

'It is the truth,' No-one Going Nowhere spluttered, the blood pouring over his head.[64] 'But it is not complete yet: this is just the first wave. Let it flow over you just as many times as the lights approached us, and curse it while it does so: only then it will be clean.'[65]

Tamar found it hard to curse something that she had no particular dislike for, but nevertheless did as her friend advised. The fifth time, she experienced a cleanliness that exceeded the other features of the blood. It was the first time she stood eye to eye with the special quality of the Hiding Place.

'Finally we have reached the gate of our death,'[66] No-one Going Nowhere said, dripping with clean blood.

'Which implies that this is only the first of ten surprises[67] awaiting us,' Tamar replied. 'Surprises that will balance out that which is above with what is below,' she added.[68]

'And equating that which is holy with that which is mundane,'[69] No-one Going Nowhere concluded.

At this point, walking the Way of the Living Tree,[70] the warlocks both felt the hand that earlier had stopped Tamar in her tracks.[71] Two gates of death opened, one for each of them, according to the double *vav*, and the double 4.[72] Without hesitation or fear the two warlocks each stepped through their own gate, about to commence on a personal journey that was entirely adapted to their specific dispositions.

The master of enthusiastic wisdom had been following their progress with interest. In the early stages of their journey he had marvelled at the quickness with which they had implemented the Sacred Number.[73] He had seen many shamans, enchanters, and even the odd alchemist make their way over the Walls of Separation,[74] but none of them had prepared themselves sufficiently for what awaited them beyond. But these warlocks! Not only had they come with the full awareness of the fifteen's glory, they had also brought with them the fruits of the necromancers' efforts.[75] They had strode straight into the waters of the Lake of the Mind's sister without letting themselves be distracted. They had even made it into Esther's Garden,[76] as he preferred to call the Secret Garden, without any major mishap. But of course, their activations had been mostly meaningful and therefore limited.[77] That was why, when they had been on the verge of pronouncing the First Name[78] in its entirety, he had intervened. The laying of his hand[79] had brought about their entry into the arena of what the warlocks themselves had termed 'the ten surprises'.[80] And although his young combatants had tamed the one-sided conception of blood and had wrapped themselves in textual reality, he knew they had missed out. For one, even though they had come close,[81] they had overlooked the matter of the blood of the five.[82] But since the truth[83] contained in Genesis 9:6 was attainable via different means as well, this was just a minor consideration. More importantly, something bigger had slipped past them too. Something so big, it was hard to see. He knew this because the forty-two lettered name[84] had told him so. It had called out to him from both sides of the 'ten surprises'[85] asking him to join the warlocks and see what he would see. It called him not just by his earthly name, but also by the name that bore the vitality of his soul's spark. There lay a promise in that call, a promise so powerfully clarifying[86] that it didn't matter that he didn't understand it.

For many reasons, not least the fact that any proper meditation entailed the exodus from opposing forces, he had expected the warlocks' next engagement to come from the seventy-two lettered name.[87] But all he could descry around the two gates now was the presence of the forty-two lettered one, blue and white, assuming the shape of a vast mountain range, emanating its wish for him to come with the full force of its mass. It gladdened him beyond measure.

Dov got up from his usual spot on the shore of the flamingo lake and picked up the clothes he had laid out to dry. Initially he had witnessed the onslaught of the blood with nothing more than mild interest, knowing that the warlocks still had to pass the stage of inversion before arriving at peaceful reality[88] beyond oppositions.[89] However, when he heard No-one Going Nowhere advise Tamar, and he scrutinised the quote underlying that advice, he was all ears. The youngster had evaded the question of what the correct counteractive of blood was by using clean blood as a side-track.[90] What's more, he had chosen a quote that had enabled him to actuate and shield all of their heart and all of their soul with equanimity.[91] He had attacked the challenge itself, and had done so from within, furthermore tying together virtually all the concepts that could be said to matter.[92] This of course had not been without effect.

After a revolving sword[93] made of dew[94] had, almost apologetically, offered itself as one example of inversion that the warlocks could have used, the matter of blood had been dispensed with, and the gates had manifested themselves.

While collecting his clothes, Dov wondered about the timing of the call he felt pulling him. He realised that all he could say about the relationship of the blood and the forty-two lettered name, was that the latter contained the former.[95] It seemed that the name's call drowned out everything else. But, to be honest, that was fine by him.

Dov walked slowly back to his makeshift shelter on the lake's shore, pausing here and there to assure himself of the consistency of the name's energy.

The spirit of the androgynous being[96] had cleansed[97] the blood and hence let the youngsters in, he knew that much. But the power he now felt emanating from the Hiding Place[98] they had been allowed entry to, could very well manifest itself to them as darkness.[99] And, if not handled correctly, they might just miss out on the bright light concealed by the clouds.[100] So he justified to himself the hurried way in which he prepared for his journey, all the time aware of course that his participation had already begun, yes, had never for a moment even been interrupted.[101]

As if to enforce this unconscious claim, Dov decided, before following the warlocks into the thick darkness[102] of Esther's Garden, to visit the temple[103] of the Thousand Faced One.[104] Dov had taken on the demanding role of being the pujari of this most western shrine in the land of the orange robes, just as, for many years on end, he had done so at one of the most eastern ones.[105] Whereas his time spent in the latter temple had reinforced his bond with the Queen of snakes,[106] his sojourn into the tribal areas of the west had intensified his interactions with the Wild Ones.[107] This, naturally, had given him ample exercise for the dealings that lay ahead.[108] So, as well as having to instruct the other priests of the temple as to how precisely to continue the worship he himself had reinstated there, he also wanted to return to the place[109] that had facilitated his departure from continuity.[110] He wanted to return to the place where the beginning of the end had shown him the truth.[111]

Dov walked the path leading him through dried up lakes where various birds waded in what little water was left. No flamingos this time, but spoonbills, herons, geese, ducks, and smaller birds eating what the lakes had given life to. It was these smaller birds that he had befriended over the years, and very useful friends they had turned out to be. He called them 'knowing birds',[112] since they had displayed the peculiar habit of knowing things that other birds didn't. Or, at least, the knowing birds knew how to communicate that knowledge to him. At best, the other birds might be seen carrying something edible to their offspring. These small birds, however, brought Dov things of an entirely different nature. Sometimes they would bring him things they had collected, placing them in front of him in such a way that suggested a completely new perspective. Other times, they would try to communicate their message to him by means of their actions. As time passed by, Dov had come to understand that everything the knowing birds did, was aimed at skilfully sowing together the fabric of mythological realities separated by physical distance only. This morning, that for all Dov knew might be the last with his winged friends for a long time, they greeted him with one of their theatricals.

As soon as he had left the hamlet that once had been thriving with pilgrims every day of the year, five little birds landed on his shoulder. Almost immediately they took off again, flying in the direction of the lake. When it was clear that they could not be heading anywhere else, they swirled back to him, only to as if drop dead in mid-flight right in front of him. They repeated this performance five times. At first Dov showed them his appreciation the way they had taught him to: by blowing one singular, elongated, plaintive note on his bamboo flute (he had discovered their affinity for this instrument when, during his daily hour of practise, two birds had alighted on the flute and with their feet closed some of its holes, playing a note that had made them and Dov sit still for the rest of the hour). Dov thought that the five birds were hinting at the lake sacred to the Gathering of the Five, the place where the warlocks had commenced their journey. Perhaps they thus wanted to bid him farewell, or even urge him on to go and see what he might see. The five birds pretending to be dead, he interpreted to imply that not only did they know about the Secret Garden, they also were informed about the fifteen letters with which the warlocks had adorned themselves. While walking on towards the temple, every now and then bringing forth a soothing, slow wave of monotonic sound from his flute as a sign of his appreciation, the deeper meaning of the birds' message struck him. Yes, the birds knew of the garden and the letters that lay at the foundation of the warlocks' journey, but they had also granted him an entrance into the reason behind the call of the forty-two lettered name. The key thus handed to him brought the realisation that there was no need to make any parting gestures to his friends the birds: creatures knowing this much would be able to join him at will wherever he went.

For the rest of his walk to the temple that for him symbolised both the dust of his body[113] and the full potential of his five-fold soul,[114] Dov rode the oceans of silver-tongued moonshine as free from intent as he had been, when deciding to give in to the call of the name. No final conclusions of clever reasoning could be ascribed to his state of mind during those final steps. Only when the master of enthusiastic wisdom reached the well-used gate of his blessed death,[115] did he return to the realm of discursive thought. Upon his return the four chambers of his heart were waiting to each offer him a piece of information. The first chamber disclosed that when he arrived at Esther's garden, he would find No-one Going Nowhere there, but not Tamar.[116] The second chamber, priding itself on being the second and hence connected to the letter *bet*, slightly distractedly pointed out that the first part of No-one Going Nowhere's name was more heavily embedded in wisdom than its nihilistic meaning would suggest.[117] The third chamber simply stated that five-fold death[118] would be the opening, would transport him instantly to the Hiding Place, and to the midst of the sweeping blue and the invincible white.[119] The last, fourth, chamber reiterated and fulfilled the message about the two systems breathing in and out like the rolling tide: it was they who were to be his tools in the presence.[120]

Then a spirit lifted Dov up[121] and transported him straight into the main shrine of the temple. He reverently touched the lingam with his forehead, changed his clothes, putting on a red longi,[122] and then sat down. Keeping out his fellow priests, who had come to see who was making the sounds emerging from the main shrine, merely by his demeanour, he lit incense and placed it around the lingam. When he was ready to instruct the priests on how to conduct his business in his absence, he called them in with the words, 'Blessed be the glory of the Lord from his place' (Ezek. 3:12).[123]

CHAPTER 3

❀

THE THREE OF ME

(The trees of) life and knowledge are not to be torn asunder from one another: they must be seen and realised in their unity.

Upon hearing the quote from Ezekiel 3:12, Dov's three chelas Lakulisa, Skanda, and Vithal[124] timidly entered the shrine. Dov's unnoticed entry to the temple had not surprised them: their guru had been known to do things far more miraculous than move about[125] unseen. What startled them, was the mood of seriousness that he appeared to be wrapped in when they approached him. Guruji had reprimanded them before when they neglected observance, but there were always clear reasons for his outbursts. On this occasion however, they were unable to fathom the immediate cause for his demeanour. They concluded that they knew even less about what moved in the depths of their master's soul than they had always presumed.

Lakulisa, Skanda, and Vithal sat down in their accustomed spots, feeling uncomfortable, and waited.

'Behold,' Dov broke the silence in what was for the three an uncharacteristically benumbed voice. 'You have driven me out this day from the face of the earth; and from your faces will I be hid; and I will be a fugitive and a vagabond in the earth' (Gen. 4:14).[126]

The prospect of seeing their honoured teacher and dear friend depart from them in such a harsh spirit alarmed the three chelas tremendously. However, just before they got the chance to protest, Dov spoke again.

'Only do not two things to me, then I will not hide myself from you.'[127]

Prepared to do anything to avoid being abandoned by their guardian, they eagerly made ready to inquire into the two things they would need to refrain from. But before they could voice their intention, their unspoken words had overruled their emotions. Returning to equanimity through the balance of the first name,[128] they recognised the performative[129] quality of Dov's speech, and hurried out to fetch the statue of the Green Queen[130] from an adjacent shrine. When they returned, they found Dov's surroundings heavily permeated by the perfume of jasmine. Their guru's body was still in its old position in front of the lingam, but they knew it was void.[131] Their master had achieved his second Small Death,[132] and they rejoiced for him.

Dov roared like a bear[133] when he saw the Garden manifest itself around him. To be absolutely sure he had arrived in the right place, he checked for judgement, but there was none.[134]

'From five times death to the elated five[135] times life[136] in the twinkle of an eye,' said the Daughter.[137]

Dov had expected her,[138] but that hadn't immunized him against the penetrating qualities of her voice.

'I but followed what was offered to me without my asking for it,' Dov replied humbly. 'Three righteous men[139] taught me how to breathe[140] in the correct rhythm; it was they who led me to the ground upon which the dead live,'[141] he explained further.

'You see clearly, son of the bears,' the Daughter said approaching him. 'Tell me what your eyes make of the third letter.'

Dov lifted his eyes and looked (Gen. 18:2). He saw a house at the beginning and a house at the end.[142] Both houses were blessed,[143] and although they were as different as formlessness and void,[144] each reflected the other,[145] and crowned together they bowed to the Name.[146]

'The third letter appears to me as both the second and as the first embedded in the last,' Dov told the Daughter.[147]

'And since one times one binds the last to the first, what is it that the five brings us, oh Seer?' the Daughter inquired further.[148]

'Five times the third beseeches us.[149] Five times the shadows of the righteous ask for permission to move freely in all directions.[150] They will carry the abundance that they have gotten to the brook of the willows (Isaiah 15:7) where Mother will await them.'[151]

'Having returned us to her[152] so gracefully, I shall follow your example. But before I leave you to your own devices, let me encourage you by saying that there is one hint left in me,'[153] the Daughter entrusted to him.

Dov watched her turn away from him and climb a ladder[154] he hadn't noticed before to the top of a golden mountain[155] that he had likewise been oblivious to. He knew that he had accomplished his first Big Death and felt strangely unimpressed by it.

With the Daughter's departure the forest of the Secret Garden assumed an air of eerie deadliness. This sensation was accentuated by a barely visible mist that settled low between the tree trunks. Like the proper understanding of the holy tongue follows from the proper understanding of the past, the crow comes forth from the evening, this Dov knew.[156] He followed the crow's flight amongst the trees with interest, and when it flew into a particularly dark part of the forest, he felt compelled to pursue it. Making his way through the gloomy blackness, he quickly learnt that this was where the owls dwelt.[157] The silent nocturnal hunters continued their business unperturbed by Dov's noisy stumbling, although Dov's temptation to question them about the legendary white owl[158] did not slip past them. Dov, however, knowing that the time was not right for philosophical discussions, bridled his tongue.[159] He wisely stretched the line of confusion upon it, barring his words with stones of emptiness,[160] and continued his descent into the realm of the shadows of death.[161] He once had known this territory well, recognising the paths leading to the dwelling of light within it,[162] but on those occasions the crow had not been his guide. The places he was led to now were far removed from any paths. Here, anger was deferred, and praise cut off.[163] When the crow had brought him so far into the absence of light that he could no longer recall either illumination or darkness, he said to Dov: 'Go forth, and stand upon the mount before *yud heh vav heh*' (1 Kings 19:11).[164]

Dov, presuming that in the pitch dark the mount was to be taken mostly symbolically, settled for standing as still as he could. Soon a great and strong wind rent the mountains (1 Kings 19:11),[165] but Dov could not detect *yud heh vav heh* in it. After the wind, an earthquake came that shook the foundations of the depths, but once more Dov found it to be empty. Then something unimaginable passed by,[166] and Dov heard its essence breaking the rocks. They shattered into five pieces,[167] in one voice exclaiming the true place of each of the forty-two letters of the name.

When all fell silent again, Dov momentarily watched the seduction. To memorise the factual nativity of those letters! To enable himself to return to that place! Then a sudden draft pulled on the branches of invisible trees, and wet autumn leaves with colours sweeter than tears of remembrance covered his eyes. Doubly blinded, Dov forgot his temptation and felt oddly overcome[168] by concern for the crow instead. Worried about its tough life in the impenetrable inkiness of the nether regions, he exclaimed, 'Who provides for the crow his food? When his young ones cry unto Abat, they wander for lack of meat' (Job 38:41).[169]

Dov's words, and in particular the avatar in their midst,[170] did not go unnoticed. The king faced the king; water flew upon water.[171] The blessing was snatched from mid air and carried away by one of the owls, most probably the white one.[172] Praise was left to exceed itself.[173] It summarised what little Dov, in his blindness, was capable of perceiving: he could trust the forty-two lettered name to see to it that the crow's young ones would become full through their parent's restraint.[174]

Giving all he had and was,[175] Dov felt life fill him and emanate from his right eye.[176] His vision faltered when he concentrated on his left eye and allowed it to naturally align with his right, but soon the two balanced out and focused on what had extended from them. Dov alighted this externalised reality and soon his feet recognized the path of the tree of life,[177] the path of the three of life. Dov withdrew himself.[178]

The inside of the brain is where Dov went. Not his brain, or anyone else's, but the communal brain. It was shaped like an upside-down teardrop, or, as Dov realized in spite of his frame of references being left behind when he withdrew,[179] like a *yud*.[180] The *yud* was lined on the inside with dry, sweet-smelling hay. It made a snug hiding place.[181] Even though, strictly speaking, Dov wasn't hiding. But the *yud* itself was.[182] Not out of secrecy or spite or anything like that. No, the *yud* was hiding out of a sense of motherly protection. Knowing itself, it knew that it was the known and the knower combined.[183] Hence, it knew all the ins and outs, which, from a perspective that was less flexible, could be crushing. Yes, crushing. As in: it could be too strenuous to live up to, if that was what one had chosen to achieve. There were too many connections, too many implications for a limited brain to comprehend. It really could succumb under the weight of it all. That is why the *yud* had secured for itself a place where it was out of the reach of any thought that presumed continuance between itself and what was beyond itself. So that those minds would be protected from its grandeur until perhaps a time or reality came that enabled them to cognise it. The *yud* had wrapped itself in isolation and retracted the biggest part of its being into the almost always neglected space of the Other. Since most beings felt the uncontrollable urge to push the Other away, this move proved to be quite successful. The *yud*, quite to its own satisfaction, needed to entertain very few guests.

Nevertheless, Dov remained with the Other for five days.[184] Of course this measurement meant nothing to him while he souled[185] there, just as his description of how it was while he was there, meant nothing to him. The *yud* and he simply were. When time returned to his reality, he found he had shifted to the smaller part of the *yud* where visitors were sometimes seen.[186] As a matter of fact, there was company present when he returned to participating in the cycle.[187]

'I see you have just spent no time in the remote pasture[188] where one's soul is nourished and one is granted the remembrance of blue dreams,' Dov's company said.[189]

Dov's brain, not completely sure yet about the place he had arrived at, and the conduct of dialogue[190] proper to it, let his tongue do the talking for him.

'Yes, the pasture that contains a fullness[191] of harvest that the hungry eats up without diminishing it,'[192] Dov heard his tongue bring out.

'Ha! I can see you are one of the beings blessed with such an amount of nothingness[193] that it cleans their blood[194] from thorns;[195] a snare swallows up their substance. Hence your tongue speaks with such clarity that it addresses matters on many levels,' his company concluded.

After this, Dov bid his company farewell and began his descent to a remote village[196] renowned for its loveliness.[197]

CHAPTER 4

❀

THE FATHERS

The foundations of the world were laid bare at the blast of breath from his throne.[198]

No-one[199] missed her when she didn't reappear after her gate of death[200] had swallowed[201] her up. To some degree it was part of the game: she herself had known that just as well as everyone else had when she had left, with much enthusiasm it must be said, her country, her kindred, and her father's house.[202] Mostly though, she had not been missed because, although she didn't reappear, she had never really left either.[203] And then, of course, there was a famine[204] in her native country, a severe one, which had provided the necessary distraction for her kindred.

No-one hadn't missed her for a different reason. To him, Tamar hadn't left at all. She had only passed on to become so full of the presence of the five that she could now be found in every death.[205] He only had to call for her in the right state of mind, and she would readily reply with a clear and somehow tempting: 'Here am I.'[206]

He was the only one who could hear this answer, and although he realized this, it didn't make much of an impression on him. He knew she had become part and parcel of him and he lacked the slowness of mind to think this extraordinary. What did make an impression on No-one was the tempting undertone of her answer. It reminded him of a deep-seated emotion he had known, and, out of a sense of guilt caused by what he thought might be lack of appreciation, had suppressed for as long as he could remember. If he had to put words to it, he would describe it as the longing to give in to the end of it all. To leave all futile strife and desire[207] far behind him and surrender to the Other.[208] If he had any images at all of what this entailed, it was fragments of reoccurring dreams, and vague memories of moments when overpowering emotions put so much strain on illusion's will to be perceived as whole, that cracks appeared in the screen of reality, and he felt light shine through.

Still, no matter how good Tamar's temptation of life beyond the cracks felt, he knew he wasn't ready to give in to it: the taste of melancholy was too strong on his tongue.[209] So he left the Other for what it was, and resumed trying to get more out of his internal companion than the three words that she had so far allowed herself to communicate. Mentally summoning her again, this time he got what he was after.

'What happened to all the males that were born in his house; aren't you one of them?' she suddenly posed.[210]

No-one roamed humble and wide after Tamar's remark: her words had struck a deep cord. Yes, he was a male, and yes, he had been born. Apparently both facts had slipped his mind completely. He had been so firmly in the hold of equanimity that his gender had retreated[211] to the realm of Ardaneshwara.[212] He had furthermore been delving so sincerely into the truths of the fifteen letters,[213] that he had forgotten about the truth of life. And wasn't that what he was originally chasing: the truth of life?[214] Sure, it may be that death was the truth of life, but he still had to incorporate death into his life, not just get stuck at death.

It was of course not the first time No-one had thought things of similar nature, and, true, what he was facing now was one of the hardest facets of the path he had embarked upon: to die to the death of life in order to live the life of death. It called for constant meditation, for the kind of lively sobriety that never concluded and was ceaselessly reborn afresh. The fathers had walked that path innocent of fear. But wasn't it written that 'the fear of God is the beginning of truth' (Proverbs 1:7)?[215] But perhaps that statement needed to be read with the emphasis on 'beginning'? Perhaps it implied that what came *after* fear would be the *rest* of truth? Realising that with this question he had come full circle,[216] he resigned himself to the fact that the path was the path, and the truth the truth. Initially the latter could be perceived as externally imposed, and the former might come to negate the latter.[217] But in the end, the end that Tamar had tempted him with, the two would be as different and as infinitely complementary as the various incarnations of *tohu* and *bohu* that he had encountered were.[218] And to ready himself for that end, No-one knew that he had to get to the bottom of his melancholy. It was his melancholy that tipped the balance of his soul towards death and away from life.[219] This imbalance could be traced back to his partiality to the pursuit of truth, and, more to the point, his identification with that truth. This attitude led to the rejection of That-Which-Is in order to keep a space open for exactly that same That-Which-Is.[220] Once No-one saw his own thought processes so clearly, it was hard to understand why he had so much trouble incorporating this insight. No-one wondered if, at the bottom of it all, in the house of death that was so like the true wilderness,[221] everything came down to the fear of losing control. Losing the grip on truth that his mind, incapable of imagining or desiring its own demise, secretly claimed to have.

'What if I was really open to truth, to life, without interference,' his mind complained, in a state of mild panic, 'only to find that I was filled so entirely that there was no space left for me?'

No-one observed that thought and understood it. He did not identify with it, and no-one was provoked at the end.[222] And how could it have been different?

Hence, No-one didn't conclude that he hadn't lived up to his name.[223] With a bit of help from Tamar,[224] he evaded inquiring whether that was good or bad, and neither did he change his name.[225] Instead, he widened his path and humbled himself.[226] Fittingly, he did so in the twilight.[227]

In response, the earth swallowed No-one up. Him and his houses.[228] His houses did not survive the ordeal and, upon resurfacing, No-one had to proceed on his own[229] to the well of nothingness.[230] Dew[231] had gathered on the old well's walls; the sun's faint light reflecting on it made for a colourful display. No-one stared in the well's mouth watching the interplay of running rainbows[232] until a sudden upward gust of air caused the dew and its rainbows to retreat.[233] No-one's view now unobstructed, he could see all the way down to the dried-up bottom of the well, and, behold, there lay a small round thing, as small as the hoar frost on the ground (Ex. 16:14).[234] Intrigued, No-one climbed over the well's edge and descended into it. It was in good condition, considering the vast number of ages since its creation, and was spacious enough for him to take a few steps on its bottom. No-one carefully picked the round thing up from the ground, and it crackled[235] as he did so. It sounded like someone clearing their throat before making a speech, or like the prelude to a bout of uncontrollable laughter.[236] It however neither spoke or laughed, but merely began to radiate with a whiteness like coriander seed.[237] Biting into the tiny round thing unexpectedly filled No-one's mouth with a pleasant taste, like that of a wafer made with honey (Ex. 16:31). Wondering what it was, he turned to Tamar for an explanation. She responded to his plea, but not in the way he had hoped. She came out to meet him with timbrels and dances, reminding him that besides her he had no son nor daughter (Judges 11:34).[238] Getting the point, No-one climbed out of the well, leaving Tamar behind.[239] Outside, the garden had reinvented itself. Green poplars, hazel and chestnut trees,[240] filled with the most vibrant of birds, stood where before only grasslands had been. He also saw fig trees that had been stripped of their bark.[241] No-one made bare his right arm in response[242] and discovered the forests of speech.[243] He understood them to be somehow connected to the stripped bark of the figs, thought that maybe they were even hewn[244] from it, but it didn't really matter. What mattered was that the time to cease all motion had not yet come and he still had some sparks to release.[245] Sparks? He wondered where that notion had come from,[246] but was almost immediately in the grip of wonder itself, regardless of its subject. He sensed this redirection of his thoughts was related to the place that would be the scene of the next uncovering:[247] the forests of speech.[248]

'Where the absence of difference between wonders and letters is unwavering,'[249] he thought he heard Tamar whisper.

'Make sure that you do not falter, not in a single letter, and not in their pronunciation,' she added as he stepped forward into the woods with the objective of freeing his captives.[250]

An otherworldly glow permanently rained down[251] in the forests of speech. The area the forests covered was so vast and their trees so substantial that this glow was the only light that the youngster[252] had with which to navigate his way. Penetrating deeper into the woods, additional assistance awaited him: now he also felt instruction[253] coming from the trees themselves. Although he received it from them, he somehow understood it didn't originate in them. The instruction came from above, and the trees were the holy channels through which it reached him.[254] The longer the youngster listened to the trees, the clearer it became to him that although they passed on many different kinds of wisdom, they were the expression of a singular power. This power was one, without plurality. The youngster realized that this singularity extended into his own situation: Tamar had not joined him in the forests.[255]

Regardless of her departure, No-one carried on, whistling plaintive[256] notes that struck the trees like so many arrows, getting stuck[257] in their trunks. Touching one of these darts of supplication[258] in passing, he found them to install in him a great sense of safety.[259] They had blended with the communicating timber, becoming towers of strength[260] themselves.

As well as imparting security, they also aided the trees in transmitting the communication from above, moulding its inherit limitlessness into more comprehensible fragments. No-one perceived the trees as massive mouths and the arrows stuck in them as wonderful instrumental strings. The former blew the breath of life over the latter, making them vibrate and turning the forest of speech into a woodland of musical messages.[261] The secrets of the forest's heart[262] were thus pleasantly shepherded[263] into No-one's consciousness. They passed though his body, reverberated in his soul, and spoke of the Essence.[264] At the end of a night spent in the embrace of arboreal mantras, No-one knew.[265] He knew that in order to free his captives, he had to understand them first.[266] He also knew that to accomplish this, he would have to enter the soul of the beast.[267]

CHAPTER 5

❀

THE SOUL OF THE BEAST

Because you have set your heart as the heart of God (Ez. 28:6).[268]

Of course no-one could ever honestly state that they were ready for the beast. This would imply some sense of knowing the beast, and the main thing about it, the thing best not forgotten, is that it is completely outside of our sphere of knowledge. Above all, though, the beast is hungry. It always has been, and always will be, hungry. And since only humankind sustains it, who of that species would really be ready to meet it?

According to all we have heard with our hearts,[269] hunger makes the beast roar a terrifying roar. We cannot imagine what this would sound like, were it to be heard by living ears. To the best of our knowledge, this happens very seldom. Normally, and this is bad enough, the ravenous beast emits its roar within the walls of the human heart. It is heard all right, but instead of ears, it is the entire being that is the recipient of its cry. It invades the very thoughts we think with, making us believe those thoughts are ours.[270] And once it has its hold on us, well, it feeds.

One of the most horrible aspects of the beast is that once it has started feeding, its prey becomes intoxicated and actually begins to help it. At first, ill at ease, almost reluctantly, it brings the beast some small offerings, tokens of feigned appreciation. But as the beast grows and infiltrates further, its prey identifies with it more and more until, frighteningly soon after its first meal, the prey has taken on all beast's needs as if they were its own. From then onward, the prey is the beast's best friend, its willing provider, and its stoutest defender. At that evolved stage, the beast no longer goes by that name; no, then it is simply known as 'I'.

I had seen them leave via the crumbled section of the western fortifications. I watched them watch the movements of the living soul,[271] and when they set sail for the Hidden Garden, I got up to return to my place.[272] There I was the host of an interesting gathering[273] at which the various parts of my soul came under the inspection of Absence.

It is difficult to put the wordless into words; perhaps ascribing names and three-dimensional bodies to these parts of my soul would simplify things. That way I could personify those parts and, as protagonists, let them go on adventures that would symbolize their interactions on the psychic and spiritual levels. But if it is all the same to you, I feel I would prefer to stay true to the five-dimensional unity of my soul.[274]

So, let me rephrase the description of the gathering I just mentioned and say that the various parts of my soul were held against the light of their nameless source,[275] to see if the light would shine through them or not. Every part revealed its internal dynamics; again something, it could be argued, that is best alluded to in symbolic ways, and again I choose to turn that option down.

There were dynamics that, in retrospect, solidified in the mind as division. Some were thus called male and female,[276] others good and bad, and to yet others the more ethereal pair of giving and withholding was ascribed. There were also dynamics that evaded even the latter division, and were mostly complementary. This was the case with calculations and their consequences. They revolted against any direction, willing to prove or disprove, taking me by the hand as confirmation while at the same time pressing my hand to convey a warning against confirmation.

To the reader it might sound like my place is extremely busy, but in fact this is not so. All activity radiating from the descriptions I have just given can be effectively hidden under one tiny leaf, and will not be found even when a gentle breeze turns it over. It could perhaps be stated that all this activity is only potential and therefore eludes the eye. Or it could be compared to the appearance of the likeness[277] of a shadow in the dark.

You follow No-one to the border of Charan.[278] He knows the name of this place, but he also knows he cannot enter it.[279] He slows down, his earlier determination drawing to an end without leaving a trace.[280] You walk up to him to join him for the remainder of his journey. Together you cross the plains and climb Mount Nebo[281] from whose peak you show him all there is to be seen. He lingers when you point the city of palm trees out to him,[282] and together you stand watching it in silence for some time. Then No-one sees noisome beasts passing through Charan, spoiling it and making it desolate, and his attitude hardens.[283] When he turns to you, though, he speaks his heart calmly and clearly: 'I, the righteous, will die here according to the statutes of the Lord.'[284] Upon this, his last speech, he falls down without any trembling, and his eyes follow his soul up almost immediately.

You bury him opposite the house of the trinity,[285] in a gap[286] hidden from the view of the beasts.[287] Then you descend[288] and cross the border into Charan, where the secret hope for eternal rest is obliterated.[289] It is the fifth day since your departure from the lake,[290] and a strong wind meets you from the north.[291]

With my next exhalation[292] what could be called the mild inner conflict between the realisation of confirmation and the gentle reminder to not restrict any processes by naming them, became almost humorously irrelevant. These notions' building blocks shrunk under the sudden light of fearless observation, and they retreated as if ashamed of themselves. At the same time I became much more aware of my blood flowing through my body. I could feel it throbbing plainly in each part of my body that

I focussed my attention on. But wherever consciousness thus settled, it quickly disintegrated into the parts of unconsciousness that it was built from.

You walk on, bent forward to brace yourself against the continually increasing wind,[293] engaged in a contest the victory[294] of which merely requires rising above the concept of failure.[295] When the hands of the poor[296] fall limp at their sides, one of the beasts that was so frightening to No-one rises from the lake in a far-from-fearsome form. This half snake, half woman stretches out her hands[297] to you and in them you discern a book.[298] You accept the good book and, applying innocence[299] with which to read, notice that your eyes alternately perceive the black letters in the book, and the white spaces they are clothed in. When both observed shapes disclose the fire at their hearts, and the words become unstuck and divorced letters take their place, you get a glimpse of the goodness and justness of the law.[300] You watch the sounds of the pompous letters that the fire is emitting. You watch without entering into a relationship with them, standing firm and keeping within motion until the beast is slain, its body destroyed and given to the burning flames.[301] Your desire to know the truth about the fourth beast, apparently different from all the others, is not diminished by this.[302] You tear your gaze away from the peoples, nations, and languages[303] falling apart in the realm of the book, and bravely stay the course, the countenance of which changes[304] with the disintegration of the instruments you navigate it with. From the ruins that you pass you can still make out remains that attest to your predecessors' descriptions. You carefully step over pieces of broken iron teeth and likewise avoid clippings of bronze nails.[305] Their urge for dominion, disguised as whispers of appropriation,[306] does not trouble you much. With time and law changed to their core,[307] you for the first time see the Secret Soul Garden that lies beyond the image of it.[308] Three kings,[309] each holding a book, see you off.

I sunk deeper into the unknown. The next breath I took cut me loose from the breaths I had taken before, opening that which appears to have no end.[310]

The creature whose kingdom[311] you now enter can hardly be called a beast, mostly because words are not permitted in its presence.[312] But even assuming time has any say, and describing it in retrospect, its form defies all similarities to what one would call a beast. You feel it is best portrayed by formlessness and stillness. However, the fierceness of wildness is not absent; it strikes you with an apocalyptic force whenever your mind offers you a composition of letters to capture some part of its being. Ignoring your mind's conditioned tendencies, you realise more and more that the fourth beast does not leave the confines of its numerical manifestation. In order to dwell safely in its wordless wilderness, and sleep unharmed in its horned woods,[313] you immerse yourself in each of the four branches of its healing waters.[314] Thus initiated, and all thought immobilised by the absence of words, you are offered a covenant of peace.[315] In actuality this materializes in a reversed manner: it is you who are the offering.[316] You offer yourself willingly;[317] each of your 248 components[318] falls freely into the womb of death that has appeared around them.[319] There is no promise of rebirth, and even if there was one, you wouldn't be interested.

Out of the midst of the lake rises the likeness of a human.[320] For a moment it seems to be surrounded by many others, but when it draws closer, I see that is not the case. There is just one being, and it is the spitting image of myself. It gently reminds me that it was I who breathed life into it and everything else,[321] and says it has now come to return my gift.[322]

Conversations
with death

Endnotes

[1] A reference to the Shiva temple of Koteshwar in Kutch, Gujarat, India, and to *To Kailash and Beyond* in general, where the number nine refers to Shiva.

[2] A reference to the five sacred lakes of Hinduism, and the five times that the word for death has been used for this novel, see *Prologue*.

[3] In Exodus 19:12, 'death', at the foundation of the trilogy (for significance of the word for death, see *Prologue*), is mentioned: 'And you shall set bounds unto the people round about, saying, Take heed to yourselves, that you do not go up into the mount, or touch the border of it: whosoever touches the mount shall be surely put to death.'

[4] A reference to other quotes in the Tenakh containing 'death' in general and to those containing the phrase 'their blood shall be upon them' in particular, for example Leviticus 20:11, 12, and 13.

[5] The verb used to express 'the blowing of life' is linshom, לנשום, which has as its three root letters the *nun*, *shin*, and *mem*. These three root letters, also spelling the word *neshamah*, 'soul', together amount to 390, which equals the outcome of 15 (the number of letters taken from the Torah as the foundation of this novel, see *Prologue*, and the number of the name *yud heh*, יה) times 26 (the number of the Tetragrammaton, *yud heh vav heh*, יהוה). For the specific godly names, see also table 1.

[6] The seals are working with the first matter, *hachomer harishon*, החמר הראשון. *Hachomer* amounts to 253, which is the number of 'created', *nivra*, נברא, explaining the creational aspect of the passage. Furthermore, the word for

time, *zman*, זמן, is made up of the letters *zayin*, *mem*, and *nun*. When writing the names of these three letters out in Hebrew (זין מם נון), one finds that their total also amounts to 253.

[7] 'Living soul' is *nefesh chayah*, נפש חיה, and has the value 453. The same number applies to 'half the Name', *chatsi hashem*, חצי השם. This is a reference to the name *yud heh* that, as the first two letters of the four-lettered Tetragrammaton, is called 'half the Name'.

[8] 'Heavens' is *shamayim*, 390, שמים, like the root of 'the blowing of life' (see endnote 5). 'Desire' is *ratson*, רצון, which shares its number 346 with 'His Name', *smo*, שמו.

[9] 'The full name', שם המפורש מלא, a reference to the Tetragrammaton, amounts to 1042. When taking the 1000 as the 1, since the word *aleph* implies both, the total is 43. 'Falsehood and truth', שקר ואמת, amounts to 1041, or 42. Hence the implication is that through the mediation of the full name, in the full name, falsehood and truth are 1: 42+1=43.

[10] Fifteen, according to the value of the name *yud heh*, יה, but also according to the fifteen letters from Genesis that provide the foundation of the novel (see *Prologue*).

[11] The name *yud heh* can be seen as half, since it is made up of two of the Tetragrammaton's four letters, but it can also be seen as containing the full name since the numerical value of the two letters, when written out fully (יוד הא) equals that of the Tetragrammaton: 26. This inherent fullness of the two letters *yud heh* is referred to by another name: *Elohim*, אלהים The letters that make up this name also spell *yud heh male*, יה מלא, meaning 'the full (name) *yud heh*'.

[12] Reference to Isaiah 26:4: 'Trust in the Lord for ever: for in the Lord Jehovah is everlasting strength.' The last part of this sentence, 'for in the Lord Jehovah is everlasting strength', יה יהוה צור עולמיסכי ב, is often read in kabbalistic literature as: 'For with the letters *yud heh* Jehovah formed (the) worlds'.

[13] Two inclinations, when taking the singular 'inclination', 300, יצר, twice, amounts to 600. This is the number of the Hebrew word for 'six', *shesh*, שש, which denotes the six days of creation. When writing the six hundred out in Hebrew, שש מאת, the value is 1041, like that of 'falsehood and truth' (see endnote 9): in essence the two inclinations are one.

[14] See endnote 9, this amounts to 1042.

[15] From the 1041 of 'falsehood and truth', via the 1042 of 'the fullness of the outstanding name', one gets to 1043 of 'that the living soul ran', שרץ נפש חיה (for 'living soul' see endnote 7). Practical kabbalists have interpreted this quote from Genesis 1:20 (there translated as 'the moving creature that has life') as an incitement to permute the letters of the Hebrew words. Through permutation, the power of the letters would be 'actuated', would be brought from their potentiality to their actuality. When looked upon like this, the first word of the quote, 'that he ran', *sherats*, שרץ, is then taken as a reference to *Sefer Yetsirah* (often translated as 'the Book of Creation', written by an unknown author somewhere in between the first and sixth century. Many kabbalists conceived this book, often ascribed to Abraham himself, as a great source text of kabbalistic secrets), where it is written: ואם רץ לבך, שוב למקום; 'when your heart runs, return to the place' (chapter 1, *mishnah* 8).

[16] The twenty-two are the twenty-two letters of the Hebrew alphabet. For 'fifteen' see endnote 10. The 'renewal' mentioned in this sentence implies 'permutation'. Practical kabbalists also used the word *chidush* to express this.

Chidush ha-22, 22-ה חידוש, 'the permutation of the 22 (letters)' amounts to 355, which also spells 'the name *yud heh*', יה שם, completing the circle to return us to the 'fifteen' of the letters *yud heh*.

[17] This gathering is that of the fifteen letters from Genesis, using the word for death, *mavet*, מות, as the guideline. It is called self-affirming, since the last three letters selected in this way are exactly the three that spell *mavet*, albeit in a different order.

[18] The 'god of death' here is a reference to the Hindu god Shiva. Within the sefirotic world, Shiva and his attribute and representation the lingam, a phallic symbol, can be said to be paralleled by the *sefirah Yesod*, itself the groom of *Malkhut*, which it penetrates and fills with its flow. This analogy is strengthened by the fact that *Yesod* is the ninth *sefirah*, and the name of the ninth letter, the *tet*, amongst others signifies the snake; Shiva is also known as the Lord of the snakes. Apart from being known as such and besides that being the god of death, Shiva is also a creator. This ties in with one of the cognomen of *Yesod*: אל חי, 'the living god'. *Yesod* however is also called *Shadai*. This name literally means 'that it is enough', and is said to be the godly exclamation that put a halt to self-expanding creation.

[19] The root of the verb 'to breathe' has 390 as its numerical value (see endnote 5). 'Male and female', *zakhar venekevah*, זכר ונקבה, also amounts to this. The electrification of the raft is a reference to Ezekiel 1:27, where *chashmal*, חשמל, is mentioned. Usually translated as amber, the word also carries the meaning electricity. *Chashmal* is used here together with 'male and female', since when one takes away the first and last letters of 'male and female', זכר ונקבה (that together spell 'this', זה), one is left with כר ונקב, amounting to the 378 of *chashmal*.

[20] Two translations of 'confrontation' are referred to. One is הקבלה, *hakbalah*,

a reference to *ha-kabalah*, 'the kabbalah'. The other is *imut*, עימות, which, when divided into 80, עי, and מות, 'death', subscribes to the earlier (see endnote 18) comparison between the Hindu god of death, Shiva, and the *sefirah Yesod* (which also has the numerical value of 80).

[21] Instead of living in the moment, he has fallen victim to the thought that certain parts of their journey are more important than others, and that those more important parts lay ahead. In effect, No-one Going Nowhere is defying the essence of his own name, and that of true knowledge: instead of working with 'received knowledge', *kabbalah*, he is imposing knowledge on reality.

[22] This quote contains the word *neshamah*, the root of which is 390 (see endnote 5).

[23] 'Balance' is *meoznayim*, מאזנים. As a sun sign this is Libra, which in Hebrew is written together with the word *mazal*, מזל. *Mazal meoznayim* has the numerical value of 225, which is the square of 'half the name' (see endnote 11): 15 times 15. The square of the remainder of the Tetragrammaton, the two letters *vav* and *heh*, is 121, which equals the name of the sun sign Aries, *mazal talah*, מזל טלה. Together these two squares amount to 346, which spells 'his name', *shmo*, שמו.

[24] A reference to the words translated as 'was left in him', *notrah bo*, נותרה בו, of 1 Kings 17:17 (see endnote 22). These two words amount to 669. 'Love', *ahavah*, אהבה, amounts to 13; together with 669 this becomes 682. This last number is the total of the fifteen letters gathered from Genesis as the foundation for this novel (see *Prologue*).

[25] In this case 'half the name' doesn't refer to the letters *yud heh*, but to

exactly half the value of the Tetragrammaton: 13. It refers to 'love' (see endnote 24).

[26] Here 'half' refers to 'half the name', fifteen (see endnote 11). 'Fullness' refers to the square: 225 (see endnote 23).

[27] The number 682 (see *Prologue*).

[28] The word for soul intended is *nefesh*, נפש. *Nefesh*, which has the value of 430, is appropriate here because of its appearance in the word *vinafesh*, וינפש, 'and he was refreshed' (Ex. 31:17). The latter conjunction has the same numerical value 446 as 'death', *mavet*, מות.

[29] The reference is to the number 682 that was the result of the incorporation of the numbers of the root letters of the word for 'death', *mavet*, as the foundation for this novel. Because of this the descriptive word 'necropolis' is used.

[30] The 'chronicles' are the myths of the Hindu temples, regarded as a fully functioning reality, 'the living sanctuaries'.

[31] Reference to Genesis 1:2: 'and the earth was formless and void', והארץ היתה תהו ובהו. 'Formless and void', *tohu vebohu*, amounts to 430, just like 'soul' (see endnote 28).

[32] The biblical Tamar had a child with Yehudah (see Gen. 38), the fifteenth generation from Adam. This in itself is a reference to the fifteen of the name *yud heh* and the fifteen letters selected for the novel. 'Tamar and Yehudah', תמר ויהודה, amounts to 676, which is the square of 26 (of the Tetragrammaton).

³³ A reference to Talmud: b.Gittin 57b: 'the words of the Torah are only realized by them who kill themselves for them in the tents of wisdom'. The singular 'tent of wisdom', when abbreviating the word for tent, אהל, is א חכמה, and amounts to 74. This is the same as the value of Hadasah (Esther 2:7), the other name of Esther. *Esther*, אסתר, also meaning 'I will hide' (a reference to the Hiding Place they will soon encounter), has the numerical value of 661. Together with the 15 of 'half the name', this 661 becomes 682. However, חכמה א also refers to Psalm 111:10: 'the fear of the lord is the beginning of wisdom'. This quote was interpreted by many kabbalists to mean that the beginning is wisdom. Both the books *Bahir* ('the Book of Clarity'; the oldest book in kabbalistic literature, written by an unknown author in the North of Spain or the Provence in France at the end of the twelfth century. It is the first book in which the kabbalistic symbolism of the ten emanated godly attributes, the *sefirot*, is formulated) and *Yetsirah* contain references to this. Finally, the phrase 'killing yourself' for the Torah was used by the so-called practical kabbalists (a division identified by G. Scholem, referring to a trend of Jewish mysticism headed by the kabbalist A. Abulafia [1240- +- 1291]), who interpreted it as a description of complete personal (physical, moral, and spiritual) cleansing, culminating in the virtual absence of the individual itself (where *ani*, אני, I, becomes *ain*, אין, 'there isn't').

³⁴ 'Name by name', *shem ba-shem*, שם בשם, amounts to 682.

³⁵ Reference to the kabbalistic view that the pronunciation of the Hebrew letters draws down their spiritual powers from above into their earthly representations. 'The work of the chariot', a reference to the vision of the celestial chariot as described in Ezekiel 1, juxtaposing *ma'aseh bereshit*, denoting the esoteric doctrine of creation, is *ma'aseh merkabah*, מעשה מרכבה, again 682.

[36] The godly name 'the Lord of Hosts' is *yud heh vav heh tsevaot*, צבאות יהוה. *Tsevaot* can also be translated as 'armies', hence 'the battle'.

[37] Now that the work of the chariot has been hinted at, the river Khebar with which the book of Ezekiel (Ezek. 1:1) opens is mentioned.

[38] They moor at the fourth branch, since the first word of Ezekiel, *vayahi*, ויהי, amounts to 31. This is the number of the name *El* traditionally ascribed to the fourth *sefirah Chesed*. This is the warlocks' first stop, since the first four of the fifteen letters they have prepared for the journey amount to 21, the value of the first part of the name of the first *sefirah Keter*: *Ehuyeh*, אהיה.

[39] The secret garden firstly refers to the Garden of Eden. Secondly it denotes the Hiding Place because of its numerological value (see endnote 33). Finally, it hints at a commentary on *Sefer Yetsirah* written by A. Abulafia (see endnote 33), called *Gan Ne'ul*, literally 'the closed/locked garden'.

[40] Auspicious since it is blessed: the name Khebar, כבר, contains the same letters as 'he blessed', *barakh*, ברך.

[41] 'Hiding Place' is *seter*, סתר, and has the numerical value 660. It is not so much affiliated to one *sefirah* specifically, as more the fruit of the transcendence of each *sefirah's* dogmatic restrictions, resulting in a state where 'love and severity are not distinguished or separated from each other' (see subtitle of chapter 1). The similarly numbered phrase 'their reward and their punishment are interchanged', גמול ועונש נהפך, subscribes to this, emphasizing the equanimity implied. The Hiding Place is 'their [the *sefirot's*] crown', *keteram*, כתרם, again with the value 660. Still, within the context of the fifteen foundation letters, the Hiding Place mostly denotes the first three *sefirot* since they are represented by the first two letters *yud heh* (15) of the Tetragrammaton. The third *sefirah Binah* stands out here

since the word *bi-nah*, בי נה, in numbers can be represented as 12-55: 12 times 55 equals 660.

[42] 'I will restore', *ashiv*, comes from the same verse (Ezek. 34:16) and has as its value 313. This matches the value of the first four generations when starting with Adam. Because of the inherent four (generations) it refers to the four corners under discussion, the first four letters gathered and the fourth branch at which the warlocks moored (see endnote 38). Furthermore 'answer/repentance', *teshuvah*, from the same root as *ashiv*, is seen as a cognomen of *Binah*.

[43] Again from Ezekiel 34:16, also a reference to the being driven away from the Garden of Eden.

[44] The hesitation stems from the fact that for many practical kabbalists, the 'unbinding of the knots', meaning the loosening of the ties (may they be material, philosophical or spiritual) with which we are bound to this reality, was the goal of their actions.

[45] No-one Going Nowhere was quoting Ezekiel, on which the 'work of the chariot' is based. The number 682 of *ma'aseh merkabah*, now, when No-one Going Nowhere is concentrating on the evasive letters, also expresses itself as 'the hiding place of the 22 (letters of the Hebrew alphabet)', *seter* 22, סתר 22, which amounts to 682.

[46] The word for the binding lying behind this remark is *akidah*, עקידה, used for the binding of Isaac (Gen. 22:9). 'The binding of one', a reference to the One that Itself cannot be bound, but whose manifestations can be subjected to this, is *akidat* 1, א עקידת. This amounts to 585, just as reverse, *hefekh*, הפך, does, when taking the special numerology of the so-called final letters (the letters *khaf*, *mem*, *nun*, *peh*, and *tsadi* that assume a different shape when

they appear at the end of a word; in this case the *khaf*, usually written as כ, has taken the form ך; in the former shape its value is 20, in the latter 500) into account. 'Reverse' refers to permutations in general, and the possible effects of binding in particular. A third candidate for the number 585 is the combined godly name *Elohim Tsevaot*, אלהים צבאות. The name *Tsevaot* is also combined with the Tetragrammaton (see endnote 36). When adding the 1 of *akidat* 1, א עקידת, to the name *Elohim*, one gets the number 87. This spells *blimah*, a word used only once in the Tenakh, in Job 26:7, where it means 'nothing'. It also appears in *Sefer Yetsirah*, where it is used to describe the sefirot, with many commentators giving their own interpretations of the meaning of this word.

[47] *Blimah*, but also a reference to the total numerical value 61 of the fifteen foundation letters, when taking only their digits into account. 61 is the value of the word *ain*, אין, meaning 'there isn't'. The word *ain* features both in the name *Ain Sof*, denoting what is beyond the highest *sefirah Keter*, and in the frequently used description of creation from nothingness: *yesh me-ain*.

[48] The name *Elohim Tsevaot* is usually ascribed to the eighth *sefirah Hod*, הוד, whose name amounts to 15.

[49] Creation from nothingness: *yesh me-ain*.

[50] Prologue to the number 32 of 'heart', *lev*, לב.

[51] See the subtitle of chapter 1.

[52] It soon turns out that the first letter of the four corners is also the *aleph*.

[53] The reference here is to a mystical diagram that contains fifteen letters per each of its 6 rows (the 15 of the name *yud heh*). The total numerical

value of all the letters in the diagram amounts to 435 (of 'the soul', *ha-nefesh*, הנפש). The four letters of the Hiding Place's four corners are the first and last letters of this diagram's first and last rows (together they amount to 22, the number of letters in the Hebrew alphabet). Implied is that the entry into the Hiding Place entails an exit from the state where discursive thought rules. This exit is seen as an exodus, which took place at the end of 430 years (Ex. 12:41); soul, *nefesh*, is 430.

[54] The name belonging to the highest *sefirah Keter*, Crown, is 'I am who I am' (see Ex. 3:14), *Ehuyeh asher Ehuyeh*, אהיה אשר אהיה. The reference here is to the first and last parts of this name, each *Ehuyeh*, amounting to 21.

[55] The first four names used by the kabbalists to denote the plagues (blood, frog, lice, and swarm [of flies], see Ex. 7 and 8) together amount to 890. 'The hand of the prince of peace' (paraphrasing Isaiah 9:5), *yad sar shalom*, יד שר שלום, also amounts to 890.

[56] 'Gazelle' is *tsevi*. In Song of Solomon 2:7 it however appears in the plural and combined form of 'by the gazelles', *bitsvaot*, בצבאות, amounting to the 501 of *asher*, 'who', from the name *Ehuyeh asher Ehuyeh*. The second part of the name of the *sefirah Hod* (fifteen in value), *Elohim Tsevaot*, is referred to.

[57] References to Song of Solomon 2:2. The thorns are those from the impenetrable hedge; the field, *hasadeh*, הסדה (in modern Hebrew this word would be spelled with a *shin* instead of a *samekh*, but in older stages of the language, with the *shin* in question conveying the same s-sound as the *samekh* rather than the sh-sound, they were sometimes interchanged) is a reference to Esther's other name Hadasah, הדסה (see endnote 33).

[58] References to the mystical diagram (see endnote 53). The diagram contains

90 letters: the letter *tsadi* has the numerical value of 90. The diagram has 6 rows of letters, divided over 5 groups: 6 times 5 is 30; the letter *lamed* has the value 30. The letters of the last row when added together amount to 40: the letter *mem* matches this value. The three letters *tsadi*, *lamed*, and *mem* thus found, together spell *tselem*, צלם, 'image'.

[59] The first letter of the diagram's first row is the *aleph*, its last is the *heh*; together they amount to the value 6 of the *vav*, the first letter of the last row. This letter together with the diagram's last, the *yud*, amounts to 16; the sixteenth letter of the Hebrew alphabet is the *ayin*. The diagram contains 90 letters; 90 is the number of the letter *tsadi*. *Ayin* and *tsadi* together make up the word *ets*, עץ, tree. When adding the last letter of the first row, the *heh*, one gets 'the tree of', *ets ha-*, ה עץ, denoting the Tree of Life, *ets hachayim*, עץ החיים.

[60] 'His shadow', *tselo*, צלו, is a reference to 'in his shadow', בצלו (Ezek. 31:17). The four letters making up this word are the beginning and ending letters of the first and last sentences of the Torah. Implied is another (see endnote 50) reference to 'heart', *lev*, 32, the two letters of which are the first and last letters of the Torah.

[61] Five times the word for light, *or*, אור, itself 207, amounts to 1035. When adding the 1 of the *aleph* that also means 'a thousand' to the 35, one gets 36, one step away from 'fulfilling the (37 of) heart'.

[62] Reference to Deuteronomy 6:5: 'And you shall love the Lord your God with all your heart, and with all your soul, and with all your might.' The word for soul in this quote is *nefesh*, 430. For 'image' see endnote 58. 'The heart' of Deuteronomy 6:5 refers to endnote 61. Deuteronomy 6:5 follows the declaration of unity of verse 6:4 'Hear, O Israel: the Lord our God is One.'

[63] The part 'and with all your might' of Deuteronomy 6:5 is left out in the paraphrasing of the quote (see endnote 62). The word for might there is *me'od*, מאד. This word amounts to 45, one more than the 44 of the word for blood, *dam*, דם, that is the first of the ten plagues inflicted upon Pharaoh and his people (see Ex. 7:20); hence the 'one extra measurement'. This extra one is also what was needed to get from the 36 (see endnote 61) to the 37 of 'the heart', *halev*.

[64] 'What is this', *mah zot*, מה זאת, has the same letters as 'it is the truth', *zeh emet*, זה אמת. Both phrases have the value of 453, just like 'living soul', *nefesh chayah* (see endnote 7), and are the next numerological step up from 452 of 'the way of the living tree', *derekh ets chayim*, דרך עץ חיים, and 'the growth of the field', *tsemach hasadeh*, צמח השדה (also see endnote 57), hence referring to the Hiding Place.

[65] The reference is to Deuteronomy 27:25: 'Cursed be he that takes reward to slay an innocent person. And all the people shall say, Amen.' The words translated as 'an innocent person' literally mean 'a soul of clean blood', *nefesh dam naki*, hence the cleansing of the blood. The first word of the quote, cursed, *arur*, ארור, amounts to 407. Five times (because of the five times that the image appeared as a raging light, see last sentences of the previous chapter) 407 is 2035, which, when taking the 2000 as the 2 (since the *aleph* can mean both 1 and 1000), is the 37 of 'the heart'. Apart from this, the quote also contains the word *lehakot*, להכות, translated as 'to slay'. This verb stems from the same root letters as the word for plague, *makah*, מכה. Finally, the word for reward in this quote amounts to 312, also the number of *shiv* (see endnote 42; *teshuvah*, from the same root as *shiv*, is seen as a cognomen of *Binah*).

[66] 'The gate of your death' is also the title of chapter 2. In Hebrew this is *sha'ar mavetcha*, שער מותך, and amounts to 1036, or 37. 'Ten plagues', *eser*

makot, עשר מכות, is made up of the same letters and has the same value. Of course the 1036 also refers to the 37 of 'the heart'.

[67] Reference to the ten plagues.

[68] Like 'the gate of your death' and 'ten plagues', 'above and below', *alion vetachaton*, עליון ותחתון, amounts to 1036. The allusion is to the transcendence of opposites that can even be found within the heart. It is said that a person knows the pull towards the evil tendency as well as to the good tendency. The heart, its two letters *lamed* and *bet* being the last and first letters of the Torah, thereby containing all of it, finds its fulfillment in rising above duality.

[69] 'Holy and mundane', *kadosh vechol*, קדש וחול, amounts to 454, the next step up after 453 of *nefesh chayah* (see endnote 64).

[70] 'The way of the living tree', *derekh ets chayim*: 452, see endnote 64.

[71] 'Hand' is written with the letters *yud* and *dalet*. When writing the names of the letters out as יוד דלת, and calculating their numerical value, one finds 454 (see endnote 69).

[72] Two gates of death have opened, referred to by the double *vav* with which 'death', *mavet*, can be written: מוות. Like this, death amounts to 452 (see endnote 70). The double 4 refers to the word for blood, *dam*, 44, but also to the first 4 generations and the first 4 plagues. The numerical value of the latter amounts to the 890 of 'the hand of the prince of peace' (see endnote 55).

[73] The number 682.

[74] The walls with which the story begins. They separate non-mythological and non-numerological reality from mythological and numerological realities.

[75] The fifteen letters based on the word for death that were selected for the book.

[76] Esther, אסתר, also means 'I will hide', *asater* (see endnote 33).

[77] Following the opinion of some of the practical kabbalists: even when one is permuting godly name with godly name, there is still a tie with meaning and therefore something to bind one to this earth and limit the mystical experience.

[78] The name of the first *sefirah Keter: Ehuyeh asher Ehuyeh*, אהיה אשר אהיה.

[79] The master of enthusiastic wisdom and the prince of peace are one and the same (see endnote 55).

[80] Without the influence of the master of enthusiastic wisdom, they would not have concentrated on the 501 of the middle part of the first name (see endnote 78): *asher*. As a result, they would not have come to experience the plagues themselves as they have begun to do now, since 501 also refers to the total numerical value of the beginning letters of the ten plagues ('the ten surprises'): דצכ עדש באחב.

[81] They did understand enough to use the five by calculating the five times *arur* (see endnote 65).

[82] 'The blood of the five' is 'the blood of (the letter) *heh*', *dam heh*, דם הא. This in itself explains why there were five floods of blood. Five times blood

is also symbolic of the five times that the Hebrew word for death has been superimposed on Genesis in order to draw the fifteen letters from it. Finally, *dam heh* is made up of the same letters as 'the human', *ha-adam*, referring to Genesis 9:6 in which this word appears three times: 'Who so sheds man's blood, by man shall his blood be shed: for in the image of God made he man.' Apart from tying in through the word for man, this quote also contains the word for blood (of the five) and that for 'the image' (see endnote 58).

[83] The truth that is referred to here is related to Genesis 9:6. The word from that quote that is translated as sheds is *shofekh*, שפך. The three letters making up this word are also the last letters of the words for beginning, middle, and end: *rosh*, *tokh*, and *sof*, ראש, תוך, סוף. This refers to two secrets. Firstly, traditionally the word for truth, *emet*, אמת, is said to consist of the first, middle and last letters of the Hebrew alphabet (the *mem* strictly speaking is not really the middle letter, since that honor should go to the 11th or 12th letter of the 22: the *khaf* or the *lamed*). Secondly, the first, middle, and last letters refer to ways that words and sentences can be permuted with, taking those letters to interchange them with letters of other words or sentences that are either positioned in the same, or in the opposite, place. Hence one can interchange the first with the middle or last letter, or the first of one word or sentence with the same of another word or sentence, etcetera, until all possibilities are exhausted. This permuting of the first, middle, and last letters only is held to be meaningless, and hence more powerful. The master of enthusiastic wisdom had no problem seeing all this, since he is also the prince of peace, 890 (see endnote 55), which is also the number of the second use of the root *shafakh*, שפך, in Genesis 9:6: 'he will shed', *yishafekh*, ישפך, when including the value of the final letter *khaf* (500) (see endnote 46). Furthermore, the letters of the word for truth, *emet*, אמת, are also found as the ending letters of the first three words of Genesis: *bereshit bara elohim*, בראשית ברא אלהים, tying in with the same godly name that is used in Genesis

9:6. Finally, all this is connected to the first name and through that to the ten plagues (see endnote 80) since the value of *Ehuyeh*, 21, when squared, equals 'truth': 21 times 21 makes 441 (of 'truth', *emet*, אמת).

[84] This name contains the first forty-two letters of Genesis, from the *bet* of *bereshit* (Gen. 1:1), to the *bet* of *bohu* ('void', Gen. 1:2).

[85] The ten surprises referred to are the ten plagues, whose first letters amount to 501. This 501, as asher, stands in the middle of the first name: *Ehuyeh asher Ehuyeh*. On 'both sides of it' is the 21 of *Ehuyeh*, together amounting to 42. The two warlocks each had their own *vav* from the word for death (see endnote 72) when written with two *vavs*, and now each has their own *Ehuyeh*, leading each of them to their own 'gate of death'.

[86] Reference to the *Bahir*, 'The book of Clarity' (see endnote 33). The second *mishnah* of this book deals with the words *tohu* and *bohu* from Genesis 1:2 (see endnote 84).

[87] The seventy-two lettered name is found in Exodus (the seventy-two letters of each of the three verses of Ex. 14:19-21). Also, the exodus took place after 430 years (see endnote 53).

[88] He is the prince of peace.

[89] Following both the books *Yetsirah* and *Bahir* that first state oppositions and subsequently offer that which 'decides between them' as the oppositions' synthesis.

[90] Instead of trying to find the proper opposite of 'blood', be it through its content or through permutations, No-one Going Nowhere simply used the adjective 'clean'.

[91] By using the five curses to arrive at the number of 'the heart', 37, implying that the Torah is beyond opposites, and denoting Deuteronomy 6:5 where the fullness of the heart is emphasized ('all of their heart') and which follows the declaration of unity of Deuteronomy 6:4 (hence reiterating that God is One; beyond opposites).

[92] The quote from Deuteronomy 27:25: 'Cursed be he that takes reward to slay an innocent person. And all the people shall say, Amen' (see endnote 65).

[93] Reference to Genesis 3:24 where a flaming sword that turns every way, to keep the way of the tree of life, is mentioned. 'Flaming' is *lahat*, להט, which like 'blood', *dam*, has the value 44. The verse also mentions the Garden of Eden, which the Secret Garden is a reference to, and the *kherubim*, which has the same root letters as the name of the river Khebar.

[94] Reference to 'the dew', *hatal*, הטל, with which the dead will be revived (see Isaiah 26:19). *Hatal* also amounts to 44. Both this word and the word for flaming could have been used to show the opposite of the word for blood, *dam*, 44. Connected to this: the warlocks passed through the gates of death, but have not died.

[95] 'In the forty-two (lettered name)', *ba*-42, equals the 44 of 'blood', *dam*.

[96] This is 'the spirit of *Elohim*'. *Elohim* is called androgynous, because in Hebrew this godly name can be seen as derived from a female singular, with the conjugation of the male plural. The name *Elohim* is significant at this point, because of its connection with the 'five (of the blood)'. Five times *Elohim* (the godly name traditionally ascribed to the fifth *sefirah*), five times 86, amounts to 430 (of *nefesh*, soul). The reference here is further to 'the power of *Elohim*', *koach shel Elohim*, כח של אלהים, amounting to the 444 of

the second plague, that of the frogs (it is the word for frog, *tsupardea*, צפרדע, that has this value). The 'spirit' that has taken the place of the 'power' is a reference to Job 37:21, where the word *ruach* has been translated as 'wind', but can also mean 'spirit': 'And now men see not the bright light which is in the clouds: but the wind passes, and cleanses them.' The *Bahir* (the Book of Clarity, see endnote 33) opens by addressing this verse in which the word *bahir* is used to mean 'bright'.

[97] Reference to the last word of Job 37:21, 'and cleans them', *vattaharem*, ותטהרם. This word has the value 660 of *seter*, Hiding Place; this is why they are allowed entry into the Hiding Place immediately upon the cleansing of the blood.

[98] Reference to the second quote used in the first *mishnah* of the *Bahir*, Psalm 18:12 (11): 'He made darkness his secret place; his pavilion round about him were dark waters and thick clouds of the skies.' The word for His secret place is *seter*, סתר, with the numerical value 660 (see endnote 97).

[99] Reference to the last of the quotes addressed in the opening *mishnah* of the *Bahir*, Psalm 139:12: 'Yea, the darkness hides not from you; but the night shines as the day: the darkness and the light are both alike to you.' This quote is posed as the one that 'decides' between the others (see endnote 89). The darkness refers to the deep darkness, *choshekh afelah*, חשך אפלה, of Exodus 10:22 which has the numerical value of 444 (of the second plague, see endnote 96). Darkness itself is a reference to the ninth plague of the same (see Ex. 10).

[100] Reference to Job 37:21, see endnote 96. In this quote, as well as 'spirit', a bright light is mentioned.

[101] Because of this his thoughts were filled with quotes and he is already incorporating the second plague.

[102] Reference to Exodus 10:22 (see endnote 99). Dov, always linked to the nine (see *To Kailash and Beyond*), enters the adventure together with the mention of the ninth plague. The ninth *sefirah* from below is Wisdom, *Chokhmah*, חכמה, Dov's rightful place (see *To Kailash and Beyond*). Wisdom is mentioned in the third *mishnah* of the *Bahir*, where the beginning (of the Torah: the letter *bet*, itself the second letter, just as *Chokhmah* is the second *sefirah* from above) is discussed. The ninth *sefirah* from above is *Yesod*, יסוד, likewise affiliated with Dov's disposition (see *To Kailash and Beyond*, and endnote 18).

[103] The word for temple is *mikdash*, מקדש, which has the value 444.

[104] Reference to the Shiva temple of Koteshwar in the most northeastern part of Khuch, Gujarat, India.

[105] Reference to *The Absence of Direction*, where, in chapter 8, *Human Skull Cups*, the protagonists spend time in a Rudra temple in Assam, India.

[106] The goddess Manasah (see *The Absence of Direction*, chapter 8, *Human Skull Cups*).

[107] Reference to the holy men of India, the sadhus, in general. In particular a reference to the three root letters *peh*, *resh*, *ayin*, which bear the meanings 'to hang loose' (the matted hair, long dreadlocks, that many sadhus have), and 'to be wild'.

[108] The root *peh*, *resh*, *ayin*, פרע, also lays at the foundation of the word *pharaoh*, and is hence connected to the ten plagues.

[109] Reference to *Sefer Yetsirah* (see endnote 15), and to the third *sefirah Binah* (see endnote 42). The place itself is a reference to the Tetragrammaton, since when one takes the square root of each of the four letters of the Tetragrammaton (100, 25, 36, 25) and adds them together, one gets 186. This is the numerical value of the word for place, *makom*, מקום.

[110] See *To Kailash and Beyond*, chapter 21, The story of the western Shaivite. A reference to the dogmatic conception of the ladder of the *sefirot* that Dov transcends in this chapter. Death as the exodus from dogmatic Wisdom. See also endnote 41.

[111] See endnote 109. The 'beginning' and 'truth' are mentioned together because of the last letters of the first three words, the beginning, of Genesis. They spell truth, *emet* (see endnote 83). Here it is written 'the truth', since *ha-emet*, האמת, has the same value 446 as 'death', *mavet. Mavet*, when read backwards, gives *tom*, תום, which, amongst others, means end. Hence 'beginning', 'end', and 'truth' are interrelated. Also of importance is the fact that the last three of the fifteen foundation letters appeared in the form and sequence of *tom*, a proper ending indeed.

[112] Reference to a division in the word for the second plague, frog, *tsupardea*, צפרדע. The division can be understood as 'a bird', *tsipor*, צפר, that 'knows', *da*, דע.

[113] Dust of the body, *afar ha-guf*, עפר הגוף, amounts to 444.

[114] Reference to 'potential of *Elohim*', *koach shel Elohim* (see endnote 96; *koach* can also mean power), which amounts to 444. The five-fold soul refers to five times the numerology of godly name *Elohim*, five times 86. This amounts to 430, which spells 'soul', *nefesh*.

[115] Reference to the title of chapter 2 and the numerological value 37 (see endnote 66): the gate is situated in his heart. The fact that, following the title of the chapter, 'your death', *mavetkha*, מותך, is called blessed, refers to two permutation systems that Dov has identified as being used from the first *mishnah* of the *Bahir* onward: the *akhbal* system (for its genesis see *To Kailash and Beyond*, chapter 10, The fruit of the palm tree) and the *akhbi* system. The latter starts with the same pair *aleph-khaf* with which the *akhbal* system starts, but its opposing row of letters runs in the more traditional opposite direction, resulting in the second pair *bet-yud* instead of *bet-lamed*. When permuting the word for blessing, *barakhah*, ברכה (addressed in the third *mishnah* of the *Bahir*), according to these two systems, the *akhbal* version delivers the number 398, whereas the *akhbi* version presents the number 68. Together they amount to the 466 of 'your death', *mavetkha*.

[116] The number 682 that is the symbol and essence of the Secret Garden without Tamar numerologically translates to 682 minus 640 (the numerical value of Tamar, תמר), which is 42. This tells us what will be waiting for Dov in the Garden.

[117] Nihilism can never be a path, since then it would no longer be nihilistic. Still, conceived as 'received wisdom', *kabbalah*, it can be said to be surrounded by attributes and cognomen. In this case this affiliated knowledge points at the first part of No-one Going Nowhere's name: no-one. When performing a similar permutation as shown in endnote 113, this is explained. If instead of taking the whole word for blessing, *barakhah*, one permutes only its three root letters *bet*, *resh*, and *khaf* according to the systems *akhbal* and *akhbi*, the first system provides the number 338, and the second 61. The number 61 brings us the words *ain*, אין, and *ani*, אני, each 61, both compiled of the same letters. Together they transfer the meaning 'I am not', *ain ani*, which conveys that of 'no-one'. The number 338 is interesting for a different reason. It is the outcome of the multiplication 13 times 26, the latter number relevant

because of its link with the Tetragrammaton, and the first because it is half that number, 'half the name' (see endnote 25). However, 13 is also the value of the word for one, *echad*, אחד, which refers to the Hebrew rendering of no-one, *af echad*, אף אחד. The extra word af has the value of 81, referring to the godly name *Anokhi*, reminding us that when God is fully realized, in a sense, human is no longer (see: *ain ani*). The implication of this reading of *af echad* is also that God is One. The letters lying at the base of the number 338 are the *lamed*, the *chet*, and the *shin*. Together they can spell the word *shaliach*, שלח, which means messenger. This is a reference to the eighth generation from Adam: Methuselah, מתושלח, a name compiled of the words *shaliach* and the word for death, *mavet*. Apart from hereby introducing the third plague (the eighth from below equals the third from above), it is also significant to remember that Methuselah was the son of Chenokh, the one about whom it is written 'and Chenokh walked with God; and he was not, for God took him' (Gen. 5:24). 'He was not' is expressed by the word *ainnenu*, which is based on *ain*, אין. Finally: Chenokh is often identified with Metatron, who sometimes goes by the name of 'the Prince of Peace' (see endnotes 55 and 72).

[118] Five times the value of the word for death, *mavet*, 446, amounts to 2230, which equals 232. This highly significant number contains the four different spellings of the Tetragrammaton, according to the four worlds *atsiluth*, *beriah*, *yetsirah*, and *assiyah* (see *To Kailash and Beyond*, chapter 3, *In the beginning*).

[119] Reference to the forty-two lettered name and the *Bahir*. In the first *mishnah* of the *Bahir*, the verse Psalm 139:12 that 'decides' between the preceding ones (see endnote 99), has as its final word *ka'orah*, כאורה. This word has the numerical value 232, hence implying the four-fold Tetragrammaton.

[120] Referring to the two permutation systems *akhbal* and *akhbi* (see endnote 115). The breathing in and out refers to the fact that these two systems start with the same pair, but in their development differ as expressed by the direction of their opposing row of letters (see endnote 115). The breathing itself refers to the root for to breathe, *nasham*, which has the value 390 (see endnotes 5 and 19). 'In the presence' refers to the penultimate word of Psalm 139:12 (see endnote 99): *kachashikhah*, כחשיכה. The numerical value of this word is 363, the same of which can be said of 'I will be in the name', *ehuyeh bashem*, אהיה בשם. As well as denoting 'the presence', *ehuyeh bashem* in itself has ties in many directions, not the least of which connects to the name of the first *sefirah Keter*, *Ehuyeh*, 21. This name of course appears twice in its full rendering, referring to the forty-two lettered name. However, when taken together with the last word of Psalm 139:12, *ka'orah*, כאורה, and, more to the point, with the number that this contains, the final reading of the verse's last two words is: 'I will be in the name 232'. This strengthens the position and importance of the Tetragrammaton, but also the importance of the four. The four of the four chambers of 'the heart' (37, but also 1036 of the title of this chapter), the four letters of both the Tetragrammaton and the name *Ehuyeh*, and the four gates of the Secret Garden. Of course the four itself also always reminds us of the fact that it contains the ten (*sefirot*, plagues, sayings, commandments, etc.): 4+3+2+1=10.

[121] Reference to Ezekiel 3:12: 'Then the spirit took me up, and I heard behind me a voice of a great rushing, saying, Blessed be the glory of the Lord from his place.'

[122] Here red refers to the Hindu god Ganesha and the number five (see *To Kailash and Beyond*, chapter 2, *Where the least of a bird's notes is never missed*). The number five in its turn refers to five times death (see endnote 118).

[123] The last part of Ezekiel 3:12 (see endnote 121). The relevance of this

quote is manifold (also see *To Kailash and Beyond*, chapter 8, *Where magic is rooted*). First of all, it is compiled of four words, referring to the four worlds (see endnote 120). More importantly, these four words each have significant values. The first word, blessed, is *barukh*, ברוך, and has the numerical value 228. This matches *ets chayim*, 'the living tree' (see endnote 64). The second word, the glory, is *kavod*, כבוד, and has the value 32 of 'heart', *lev* (see endnotes 50, 60, and 63). The third word, the Lord, the Tetragrammaton, speaks for itself. The final word, from his place, *mimkomo*, ממקומו, amounts to 232 (see endnote 118). The word for place, *makom*, in itself also refers to the Tetragrammaton (see endnote 109), as well as to *Sefer Yetsirah* (see endnote 15). The first letters of each of these four words taken together amount to 72, which is the number of the Tetragrammaton's spelling according to its placement in the *sefirah Chokhmah*, the second *sefirah*. Furthermore, *Chokhmah* is the beginning (see endnote 102), which is a proper concept to invoke now that Dov stands on the threshold of his more active participation in the journey of the warlocks and his dealings with the forty-two lettered name. The additional implications of the various possible permutations of these four words from Ezekiel 3:12 would render enough material for an entire book and will therefore not be included at this point.

[124] The three chelas (students) are protagonists in the chapters 5 (*The advent of strength*), 6 (*The soul of silence*), and 9 (*They sleep on the wind*) of *The Absence of Direction*. The fact that there are three of them refers to the commencement of the dealings with the third (plague, *sefirah*, letter of the fifteen foundation letters).

[125] The Hebrew verb intended is *lehithalekh*, להתהלך. This verb is used in connection with Chenokh, the seventh generation (see endnote 117) from Adam.

[126] The ninth word of this verse dealing with Cain's response to his punishment for killing his brother Abel is the word *esater*, אסתר. This word can also be read as Esther, which is written in exactly the same way, and is therefore a reference to the Secret Garden (see endnotes 33 and 76). Three verses after this one, the birth of Chenokh is mentioned.

[127] Job 13:20: 'Only do not two [things] unto me: then will I not hide myself from you.' Like Genesis 4:14, this verse contains the word esater. Both verses also contain the word *mipanekha*, מפניך, literally meaning 'from your face'. This word has the numerical value of 680, which in conjunction with the letter *bet* that means 'in', would equal the number 682 of the fifteen foundation letters of this novel.

[128] The godly name associated with the first *sefirah Keter*: *Ehuyeh asher Ehuyeh*, אהיה אשר אהיה. The first and third words of this name are now looked upon as the two scales of the balance that make for equanimity. The middle word *asher* with the value of 501 again refers to the ten plagues (see endnote 80), denoting the subject that Dov will have to deal with, will have to be equanimous about. The number 21 of *Ehuyeh* is also the first word of Job 13:20, the second of which is 'two': *Ehuyeh* appears twice in the first name. This two however also introduces the discussion of the *bet*, the second letter of the alphabet, but the third of the fifteen foundation letters. Furthermore, esater of the two verses Genesis 4:14 and Job 13:20 amounts to 661. Together with the 21 of *Ehuyeh*, this adds up to 682. In addition to this, 21 is the total of the three letters *yud heh vav* that make up the Tetragrammaton. Here, these three letters also refer to the first three *sefirot* and the third plague, leading to the fourth, which at the same time is the fourth letter of the Tetragrammaton, the second *heh*.

[129] Dov is not merely citing quotes, he is reciting them as part of a technique that in essence is magical and hence performative: what he says will come

about. Here the axis is the word *esater* through which Dov transports himself to the Garden.

[130] Reference to goddess Mukambika, who in *To Kailash and Beyond* (chapter 2, *Where the least of a bird's notes is never missed*) is placed as the third (and is therefore connected to *Binah*).

[131] Reference to *tohu* and *bohu*, 'formless and void', of Genesis 1:2. In this novel, these two words were first interpreted as the two archetypal components that are balanced out in, and make for, creation. The development, implementation, and actuation of these components, also symbolized by the various words that share their numerical value with that of the relevant plague, will lead a person to equanimity and transcendence. In this chapter this thought will be developed and expanded, based on the remarks as found in the *Bahir*.

[132] The second of the fifteen foundation letters has been dealt with. The cognition of each of the fifteen foundation letters is seen as a spiritual development. However, since the fifteen letters are the result of five incorporations of the three lettered word *mavet*, death, each completion of three letters is called a Big Death, whereas the other cases bear the title Small Death.

[133] A reference to the meaning of the word *dov* in Hebrew: bear. In the garden, the name is the thing it refers to. It is also a reference to Isaiah 59:11: 'We roar all like bears, and mourn sore like doves: we look for judgment, but there is none; for salvation, but it is far off from us.' The word for doves, *kayonim*, כיונים, bears similarity to the word for the third plague: *kinim*, כינים (in the Torah written with only one *yud*, but, following A. Abulafia [see endnote 33] here written with two).

[134] Reference to Isaiah 59:11 (see endnote 133), and to equanimity: when love (*Chesed*, the fourth *sefirah*) and judgment (*Geburah*, the fifth *sefirah*) are balanced out, neither of them can be distinguished from the other.

[135] 'The five/*heh* is the rise, ascent', *heh alliyah*, ה עלייה, amounts to 130, like the name of the third plague, *kinim*, when written out fully (see endnote 133). This phrase refers to the five times the word death has been used to bring forth the fifteen foundation letters of the novel. Here this reference is part of the description of the 'five times life', pointing at the fact that life and death are thoroughly interrelated.

[136] 'Five times death' amounts to 232 (see endnote 118), anchoring itself firmly in the Tetragrammaton. 'Five times life', when understanding 'life' to be contained in the same Tetragrammaton, amounts to 130: 5 times 26. Both life and death now point towards the third plague that has the same numerical value.

[137] Dov is addressed by the daughter for a number of reasons. First of all, the letters that make up for *tohu-bohu*, תהו בהו, 'formless-void', can be rearranged into *bat heh heh vav vav*, בת הה וו. The last four letters amount to 22: *tohu-bohu* hence also implies bat 22, or 'the daughter of 22' (letters of the Hebrew alphabet). This reading of *tohu-bohu* against the background of other topics central to the novel is subscribed by both the *akhbi* and *akhbal* systems. Permuting the Tetragrammaton through the *akhbi* system, the outcome amounts to 22 (tying in with what was said in endnote 136). Permuting the same through the *akhbal* system, the result amounts to 390, which equals 15 times 26 (see endnote 5). Secondly, the daughter refers to the first *heh* of the Tetragrammaton, traditionally ascribed to *Binah*, the third *sefirah*. The *heh* is significant because of the 'five times death/life'. Thirdly, the daughter *Binah*, בינה, implies the multiplication 12 times 55, tying in with the Hiding Place (see endnote 41), and the 22: the 682 of the fifteen letters minus 660

gives 22. Finally, there is a strong link with the *Bahir*, which, as was pointed out earlier (see endnotes 86, 96, 98, 99, 102, 115, and 119) in its opening *mishnayot* deals with *tohu* and *bohu*, the letter *bet*, 'blessing', 'Hiding Place', etc. In *mishnah* 3 of the *Bahir*, one finds a parable relating a king who gives his daughter to his son. The word for daughter, *bat*, is made up of the same two letters as *bet*, the word for the letter b. The word for son, permuted through the two systems *akhbi* and *akhbal* gives the letters *bet*, *lamed*, *yud*, and *resh*: *bli resh*, בלי ר. These four letters can be read as 'without the *resh*'. *Resh*, when read as the similarly spelled *rosh*, means 'head', or 'beginning'. Taking the first word of the Torah (the 'head', the 'beginning'), *bereshit*, בראשית, 'without the *rosh*, ראש, one is left with the first and the last two letters of the word *bereshit*, בראשית: *beit*, בית. This word means both 'house', and (the letter) *bet*, which confirms the importance of *tohu* and *bohu*, whose first letters spell this letter, and explains why the Torah opens with it. At the same time this refers to the daughter *Binah*, whose name starts with the *bet*.

[138] Dov knew that he would be dealing with the forty-two lettered name (see endnote 116); the daughter is linked to this (see endnote 137).

[139] One of the words meaning 'true/righteous men' in Hebrew is *kenim*, כנים, as it is for example used in Genesis 42:11,17. *Kenim* is a reference to the third plague, that of the lice, pronounced *kinim*, but often also written without the first *yud* as כנים. Three times (since it is written 'three righteous men') the 130 of *kinim* (when written with two *yuds*: כינים) amounts to 390 (see endnotes 5, 9, 19, and 137). The three men are also a reference to Genesis 18:2: 'And he lift up his eyes and looked, and, lo, three men stood by him: and when he saw them, he ran to meet them from the tent door, and bowed himself toward the ground' (also see *To Kailash and Beyond*, chapter 7, *The ladies of the canyon*). The first word of this verse, the word for 'he lifted up', *yisa*, ישא, also spells 'man', *iesh*, איש; and the three men in this

verse are called *anashim*, אנשים. Both words *iesh* and *anashim* are taken to refer to the third generation of Enosh, אנוש.

[140] The root of the verb 'to breathe', *nasham*, amounts to 390.

[141] Reference to 1 Samuel 20:31: 'For as long as the son of Jesse lives upon the ground, you shall not be established, nor your kingdom. Wherefore now send and fetch him unto me, for he shall surely die.' 'The ground upon which the dead live' denotes the reality where the dead and the living are one and the same, because of the understanding that mystical death leads to real life (see also *To Kailash and Beyond*, chapter 22, *The unseen sight*); this implies the transcendence of opposites. In this verse, the words for 'the son of Jesse lives', *ben jesse chai*, בן ישי חי, amount to 390. The verse ends with the words for 'he shall surely die', *ben mavet hu*, בן מות הוא, which, when taken literally, means 'he is the son of death'. Hence 'the son of Jesse lives' and 'he is the son of death' can be seen as pointing towards the transcendence of opposites.

[142] The word for house in Hebrew is *beit*, בית, which can also be written without the vowel *yud*, and then means '(the letter) *bet*' (see endnote 137). Hence, 'a house at the beginning and a house at the end' can also refer to the letter *bet* at these positions. In this latter case, this points at the forty-two lettered name, which indeed has the *bet* as its first and last letters. Of course, the realm is still that of the third, and the *bet* is the third of the fifteen foundation letters of this novel.

[143] A reference to the *akhbi* system which was discovered by looking at the three root letters of the two words 'he created', *bara*, ברא, and 'he blessed', *barakh*, ברך. The only difference between these two words in Hebrew is their last letters. Taking them as a pair of a permutation system, *akhbi* is born. The two words at the foundation of this system therefore also imply that

creation is a blessing. It is furthermore a reference to the *akhbal* system, since, as in the case of the *akhbi* system, the outcome of the permutation of the two letters *bet* and *tav* (that make up for the name of the letter *bet*) is the letters *yud* and *lamed*. It is this double appearance of the pair *yud-lamed* that is intended with the two houses that are blessed. Finally, leaving the pair *yud-tav* aside (being the pair that made for the genesis of the *akhbal* system; see *To Kailash and Beyond*, chapter 10, *The fruit of the palm tree*), one is left with the letters *bet* and *lamed*. Apart from spelling the word for heart, *lev*, and being the first and last letters of the Torah (a house in its own right; see endnote 142), these two letters are also special since they are the only two in the Hebrew alphabet to whom the letters *yud*, *heh*, and *vav* of the Tetragrammaton can be suffixed. In addition, their combined value 32 refers to *Sefer Yetsirah* that opens with the 32 paths of wisdom. These 32 paths point to the 32 times that the name *Elohim* was used in the account of creation in the first chapter of Genesis. The 32 paths can be divided into the 10 digits and the 22 letters of the Hebrew alphabet. The former are connected to the 10 times that the word *Elohim* appears in conjunction with the word *vayomer*, 'and He said' (the so-called ten sayings with which the world was created, see endnote 204, and chapter 9, *The Fathers*, in general), and to the 10 *sefirot*. The latter 22 are subdivided into 3 (times that the word *Elohim* appears in conjunction with 'He made', referring to the three mothers), 7 (times *Elohim* appears together with 'He saw', referring to the seven letters that have two ways of being pronounced), and 12 (the rest of the letters).

[144] So far the opening verses of the *Bahir* have been interpreted as pointing towards equanimity which can be reached by taking the 'deciding' verses that follow the seemingly contradicting ones as the synthesis of opposites (see endnotes 96, 99, 120, and 131). The idea behind this is that although creation is understood as founded on two main constituents (in Hinduism Shiva, divine consciousness, and Shakti, divine energy; in Jewish mysticism

the right and left columns of the tree of *sefirot*, with the middle column 'deciding' [see endnotes 89, 99, and 119] between these opposing forces of, respectively, love and judgment. Here the two forces are transposed onto *tohu* and *bohu* of Genesis 1:2 where the account of creation is given), from the human perspective, their essence remains unknown (in Jewish literature, the interpretations of the phrase *tohu ve-bohu* are manifold, since they evade one clear translation/interpretation), but considered as opposites.

[145] Although *tohu* and *bohu*, following the train of thought set out in endnote 144, are different archetypal forces of creation, they reflect each other through the application of the permutation systems *akhbi* and *akhbal*, where their opening letters give the same result (see endnote 143).

[146] The two forces *tohu* and *bohu* stand at the beginning of the process of creation. Therefore they are placed in the first *sefirah Keter* and relate to its name *Ehuyeh asher Ehuyeh*. The first and third words making up this name are externally identical, which, in a way, can be said of *tohu* and *bohu* as well (the translation 'formless and void' is an example of this: from the human perspective only words can make sense of these forces, but in essence they are meaningless, beyond comprehension, just like the highest *sefirah Keter*, which, according to kabbalistic tradition, cannot be attained or understood. Hence they are similar in meaninglessness, but essentially still different. Another example of linguistic similarity that really contains a big difference is found in the Tetragrammaton, whose second and fourth letter is the *heh*. These two *hehs* are nevertheless interpreted as very different in nature, being ascribed respectively to the third and tenth *sefirot*). Another correspondence between *tohu* and *bohu* and the name *Ehuyeh asher Ehuyeh* lies in the forty-two lettered name. While all of the word *tohu* and the first letter of the word *bohu* are part of this name, the two externally identical parts of the name *Ehuyeh asher Ehuyeh* numerologically amount to 42. Hence the two 'houses' are crowned: *Keter* means 'Crown'. In addition to this, the *akhbi* and *akhbal*

permutations of *tohu* and *bohu* amount to 366, a number spelling 'the name *yud heh vav heh*', *shem yud heh vav heh*, שם יהוה. Finally, the bowing itself is a reference to the third *mishnah* of the *Bahir*, where the word for blessing, *barakhah*, ברכה, is compared to the word for (the bending of the) knee, *berekh*, ברך, made up of the same three root letters.

[147] The third of the fifteen foundation letters of this novel is the *bet*, which is also the first letter of the third *sefirah Binah*. The *bet* is the second letter of the alphabet and the first letter of the Torah. It is also the last letter of the forty-two lettered name.

[148] One is *echad*, אחד. This word is made up of three letters with the numbers 1, 8, and 4. When squared, these numbers become 1, 64, and 16, together amounting to 81. This is the first implementation of 'one times one'. The outcome 81 is, however, also the value of *Anokhi*, אנכי, one of the names of God, the ultimate One. Incorporating this One, the 'one times one' becomes 81 times 81: 6561. When dividing this number right through the middle, one finds 65 one the one side, and 61 on the other. 65 is the value of the name *Adonai*, אדני, ascribed to the last *sefirah Malkhut*; 61 is the value of *ain*, אין, referring to what is supposed to be beyond the first *sefirah Keter. Ain Sof*, literally 'without end', but really implying the complete absence of any attribute and totally beyond human attainment. Whereas the two words making up *Ain Sof* can in themselves be looked upon as the prototype for the division needed for material creation, as a precedent for *tohu* and *bohu*, the positioning itself of the numbers 65 and 61 is also instructive. With *Ain Sof* preceding the tree of sefirot, and *Malkhut* being the last *sefirah*, these two numbers install a sense of completion. Hence: 'one times one binds the last to the first.' In his answer to the question preceding the Daughter's inquiry, he mentioned the third, the second, the first, and last. Having just dealt with the first and the last, the second and the third remain. The 2 and 3 together amount to 5. This is a reference to the second

heh of the Tetragrammaton, placed in *Malkhut*. Earlier (see endnote 128), Dov had arrived at the number 661 through quotes from Genesis and Job. Subtracted from the founding 682, he was left with 21, reflected by the first three letters of the Tetragrammaton. What was left is the last letter *heh*, which is now unearthed. Of course the five again refers to the five times that the word for death, *mavet*, was used for this novel.

[149] A reference to Exodus 8:12-14 (Ex. 8:16-18) where the *third* plague, the lice, is mentioned *five* times in *three* consecutive verses.

[150] When in the state of equanimity that is at the core of the Hidden Garden, good and bad lose their meaning. Hence the 'badness' of the lice is no longer valid, here illustrated by the 'righteous' that have the same numerical value as 'lice' (see endnote 139).

[151] The third word of Isaiah 15:7, translated as abundance, is *yitrah*, יתרה. This amounts to 615, which equals the total number of the five different renderings of 'lice' in Exodus 8:12-14 (see endnote 149). When subtracting 615 from the founding 682, one is left with 67, the value of *Binah*, Mother. Hence the link between the third and the five, as posed in endnote 149, is confirmed. The last word of Isaiah 15:7 in its Hebrew original is that for 'shall they carry away', *yisa'um*, ישאום. This word amounts to 357, which matches that of the third generation of Enosh (see endnote 139). Finally, the brook mentioned in this verse refers to the four rivers that flowed from Eden, introducing the passage to the fourth.

[152] 'Return' is a cognomen of *Binah*.

[153] 'There is one allusion in me', *remez echad bi*, רמז אחד בי, amounts to 272, which is the value of the fourth plague (see Exodus 8: 17 [21]), the swarms (of flies), in singular (swarm) *orev*, ערב. The number 272 is also present in

Isaiah 15:7, where the three root letters of the word for willow, *aravah*, ערבה, have the same value. Finally, the word *aravah* also carries the meaning desert, referring to *tohu* and *bohu*.

[154] 'Ladder' is *sulam*, סלם, which shares its value 130 with the third plague.

[155] Reference to Mount Sinai, סיני, with the same value 130 as the third plague.

[156] This passage occurs in *The Absence of Direction*, chapter 7, *The white owl*. It contains various renderings of the root *arav*, ערב, with the value 272, of the fourth plague (see also *Behind the scenes* in *The Absence of Direction*): holy tongue/Hebrew, עברית; past, עבר; crow, עורב; and evening, ערב. In *The Absence of Direction* No-one Going Nowhere is the protagonist of this passage.

[157] Reference to Isaiah 34:11: 'But the cormorant and the bittern shall possess it; the owl also and the raven shall dwell in it...' 'Raven' and 'crow' can be denoted by the same word in Hebrew, hence this refers to 272 of the fourth plague. Owl is *yanshuf*, ינשוף, and amounts to 446, sharing this number with the word for death, *mavet*. Cormorant, *ka'at*, קאת, amounts to 501, referring to the ten plagues (see endnote 80).

[158] Reference to *The Absence of Direction*, chapter 7, *The white owl*.

[159] Reference to *Sefer Yetsirah* 1:3, where the *sefirot* are described as *blimah*, the interpretation of which contains the word for 'to bridle'. 'Tamar' becomes 'tongue' by permuting it with the *akhbi* system. The main reference intended, however, is to the next step in the development of the idea of equanimity as found in the *Bahir*. *Tohu* and *bohu* now also contain an allusion to the two constituents 'giving' and 'withholding'. This corresponds with the division

of the tree of *sefirot* into columns. Its right column is the giving force, and its left the withholding force. *Blimah* is the withholding force.

[160] Paraphrase of the continuation of Isaiah 34:11 (for first part of this verse see endnote 157): 'and he shall stretch out upon it the line of confusion, and the stones of emptiness.' The words in Hebrew used for confusion and emptiness are *tohu* and *bohu* respectively. A further reference is to the new development of the meaning of these words as discussed in endnote 159. Here, 'giving and withholding' are termed 'stretching (out) and barring'. Further implied is a verse that will shortly be addressed: Isaiah 48:9, in which the 'giving and withholding' find yet another expression.

[161] Reference to Job 38:17: 'Have the gates of death been opened to you? Or have you seen the doors of the shadow of death?'

[162] Reference to Job 38:19: 'Where is the way where light dwells? And as for darkness, where is the place thereof?' Also implied are the quotes with which the *Bahir* opens (see endnotes 98 and 99). Finally it is a reference to the 'thirty-two paths of wisdom' with which *Sefer Yetsirah* opens.

[163] Reference to Isaiah 48:9 as announced in endnote 160: 'For my name's sake will I defer my anger, and for my praise will I refrain for you, that I cut you not off.' The idea of creation being founded on the two forces of giving and withholding is expanded upon. Although from the English translation of this verse it seems that it contains only verbs exemplifying the withholding aspect (the verbs 'to defer', 'to refrain', and 'to cut off'), in the Hebrew rendering there is more to it. The first verb 'to defer' in Hebrew is composed of two words that compile a saying. The verb proper is the first part, literally meaning 'to lengthen', whereas the other part literally means 'my nose', but also can imply 'breath' (hence it is a hidden reference to breathing, *linshom*, and soul, *neshamah*, that both stem from the root

nasham, 390. When in Genesis 2:7 God installs life in Adam, he does so by blowing life [*nishmat chayim*] into his nose). Hence the 'lengthening of the breath' implies the verb 'to defer', with the nose being the organ of anger that is being bridled. Therefore, when one takes only the first word of this composite verb into account, one is left with 'I will lengthen', *a'arikh*, אאריך. This is much closer affiliated to the aspect of giving than to that of withholding, and actually reminds one of the 'stretching out' of Isaiah 34:11 (see endnote 160). In addition to this, the word *a'arikh*, אאריך, has the numerical value of 232 (see endnotes 118-120), tying in with the Tetragrammaton, the topic of death, and the first *mishnayot* of the *Bahir*. Together with the second word of this verse that means 'my name', it gives us 'my name is 232'. This subscribes to the reading 'I will be in the name 232' found in Psalm 139:12 (see endnote 120), and 'my name is *yud heh vav heh*' discovered through the *akhbi* and *akhbal* permutations of *tohu* and *bohu* (see endnote 146). For all these reasons it can be stated that 'to defer' refers to equanimity, since it also entails all these positive aspects reflecting 'giving'. Similarly, the last word of Isaiah 48:9, meaning 'I will cut you off', *hekhritekha*, הכריתך, has a counterbalancing positive meaning hidden inside. It is found in its root letters *khaf*, *resh*, and *tav*, which also spell *Keter*, the name of the highest *sefirah*.

[164] 1 Kings 19:11: 'And he said, Go forth, and stand upon the mount before the Lord. And, behold, the Lord passed by, and a great and strong wind rent the mountains, and brake in pieces the rocks before the Lord; but the Lord was not in the wind: and after the wind an earthquake; but the Lord was not in the earthquake.' This verse is also mentioned in the *Bahir*. Its ninth word is *over*, עבר, matching the numerical value 272 of the fourth plague.

[165] The word for great here is *gedolah*, גדולה, which is another name for *Chesed*, the fourth *sefirah*. The word used for wind is *ruach*, רוח, which also means soul, referring to *nasham*, 390. Through *akhbi*, *ruach* becomes *nud*,

referring to 'and vagabond' of Genesis 4:14 (see endnote 126) that contains the same letters.

[166] The word for 'passes by' from 1 Kings 19:11 is over, which through *akhbal* gives the number 42, referring to the forty-two lettered name.

[167] The word for rocks in 1 Kings 19:11 is *sela'im*, סלעים, amounting to 210. This is also the numerical value of the fourth generation Cain, קינן, aligning with the fourth plague that the story has reached. Moreover, this verse contains five mentions of the Tetragrammaton; dividing 210 by five, one gets 42.

[168] Introductory reference to the word *male*, מלא, 'to become full'.

[169] The rendering of Job 38:41 has two slight differences compared to the standard translation. One: instead of the crow, in the standard translation it reads raven, which is the same word in Hebrew. Two: where the original text reads 'cry to God', here it reads 'cry to *Abat*'. *Abat* is a reference to a permutation system in which the first letter of the alphabet finds as its permutation the same *aleph*. After this, the original row of twenty-two letters runs up (*aleph, bet, gimmel*, etc.), and its permutation row runs down (*aleph, tav, shin*, etc.). Hence the first two pairs of this system are *aleph-aleph* (a-a) and *bet-tav* (b-t): *abat*. The reason why the *abat* system is brought forward here is the double mention of the Hebrew word *el* in Job 38:41. In the *abat* system, the *aleph* and the *lamed* remain unchanged, thereby providing us with two pairs of letters spelling *el*. The *abat* system found its genesis in the verse Deuteronomy 33:23 that is mentioned in the *Bahir*: '… and full with the blessing…', *umale bircat*, ומלא ברכת (see endnote 168). Since it was stated in the *Bahir* that the *bet* itself is the blessing, one could use the two letters that make up for the name of the *bet* as a pair of a permutation system. Taking it from there, one easily identifies the *abat* system. When

permuting the word for blessing used in this verse, *bircat*, with the *abat* system, the number 446 of the word for death, *mavet*, that is so central to this novel is reached. If this is not enough confirmation of the suitability of this system in the current framework of ideas as posed in this novel, one could further permute the word for full, *male*, מלא, of the same phrase. The outcome is *khaf, lamed, aleph*. These three letters in this order bear both the meanings 'to be full' (hence referring to its original meaning, and implying giving), and 'to restrain' (referring to the withholding), further confirming the system's relevance. The letters *khaf, lamed,* and *aleph*, however, also spell the word *akhal*, which is the root of the verb 'to eat', referring to, and tying in with the food, *okhel*, that is the last Hebrew word of Job 38:41 that was chosen to introduce this system. Furthermore, the 'to wander' of Job 38:41 is of the same root as 'fugitive' of Genesis 4:14 (see endnotes 126 and 165), one of the verses recited by Dov as a magical means to transport him to the Garden. Finally, the *abat* system, through its two unchanging pairs *aleph-aleph* and *lamed-lamed* refers to the fourth that is now being dealt with: the name traditionally ascribed to the fourth *sefirah Chesed* is *El*, made up of the letters *aleph* and *lamed*.

[170] The avatar being the *abat* system.

[171] The facing refers to the pairs of the permutation systems that face each other. Using the *abat* system, the word for king, *melekh*, remains the same (the letters are the same, just in a different order). The same is the case with water, *mayim* (in this case the letters change, but the numerical value 90 of *mayim* remains the same after the permutation). *Mayim* is a cognomen of *Chesed*, the fourth *sefirah*, whose name is *El* (see end of endnote 169). In addition, the fourth *mishnah* of the *Bahir* (that mentions Deuteronomy 33:23 which contains the 'fullness of blessing'), also uses Proverbs 8:30: 'Then I was by him, as one brought up with him: and I was daily his delight, rejoicing always before him.' In this verse the word *ehuyeh* is mentioned

twice, referring to the highest *sefirah Keter* (and through it, the King), and the forty-two lettered name (two times *ehuyeh* amounts to 42).

[172] Reference to the value of the *abat* permutation of the word for blessing in Deuteronomy 33:23 (bircat): 446 of 'owl'.

[173] Praise exceeds itself by means of the *abat* system. Through it, the value of the word for praise (as featuring in verses used by the *Bahir* in its fourth *mishnah*: Isaiah 48:9 and Psalm 145:1), *tehilah*, תהילה, is 232 (see endnote 163). From mere praise, it becomes the value of the four different spellings of the Tetragrammaton. The *abat* system turns the Tetragrammaton itself into the number 340 of name, *shem*, שם (see second half of endnote 163). This can be taken as a further confirmation of the validity of this system, since in *Bahir* 5 the second mention of the phrase 'full with the blessing' from Deuteronomy 33:23 (the verse that gave us the *abat* system [see endnote 169]), is followed first by the Tetragrammaton, and then by the word ומשם. This can be read as 'and from the name', suggesting that the preceding Tetragrammaton is referred to. Hence *shem* is substituting the Tetragrammaton as it also does through permutation by the *abat* system.

[174] Reiterating what was pointed out in endnote 169. 'To become full' and 'to restrain' are analogous to 'to give' (the natural aspect of God's giving is in kabbalistic texts often explained through the comparison with something that is full to the brim and hence naturally flows over and gives) and 'to withhold', the two forces lying at the base of creation which is exemplified by the outcome of permutations using the *abat* system.

[175] When giving all one is, one becomes empty, or absent. The imperative of this action for a mystic is reflected by the permutation of 'I', *ani*, אני, which through *abat* becomes 'there isn't/not', *ain*, אין. The two words contain the same letters, emphasizing the fact that the true I is the state

where the personal I is exchanged for the cosmic I or God. The *sefirah* that most strongly expresses the giving is *Chesed*. Now that Dov has given all he is, he will move on to the next *sefirah*, which is *Geburah*, Strength. These two sefirot are the prototype of giving and withholding in kabbalistic terminology. *Geburah* is the fifth *sefirah*. (The fifth of the fifteen foundation letters of this novel is the *yud*).

[176] The flowing waters mentioned in the fourth *mishnah* of the *Bahir*, are called *mayim chayim*. They flow forth from a spring, *mayan*, מעין. Instead of taking the latter word as one entity, one can also take it to contain the word *ayin*, עין, preceded by the letter *mem*, מ, meaning 'from'. Doing so, it now reads 'from the eye', thereby changing the parable from the *Bahir* as well. This now no longer speaks of flowing waters that come forth from a well, but of flowing waters that come forth 'from the eye', *me'ayin*, מעין. All this as a prologue to a simple permutation. When using the *abat* system to permute the word for eye, the outcome is *cheni*, חני, meaning 'my favor'. In this case the favor would be the flowing waters. *Cheni* amounts to 68, which it shares with the word *chayim*, used in the same passage to indicate the living, flowing aspect of the waters. *Chayim* however also means life, hence the life that emanates from Dov's eye.

[177] Reference to the title of this chapter, *The three of me*. The three of life that is spoken of are giving, withholding, and human that is made up of these two forces. The three also refer to the first three *sefirot* that are seen as the intellectual trinity of the tree of the *sefirot* ('the tree of me'). The other three indicated here is that of the three root letters of the word for death, on which the novel is based.

[178] The withdrawing refers to the withholding. It however also points to the idea of *tsimtsum*, צמצום, laid down by Isaac Luria (1534-1572; founder of what became known as Lurianic Kabbalah). It is the thought that prior

to creation, God contracted Himself, withdrew Himself, to make space for creation. Luria linked this process with the fifth *sefirah Geburah*.

[179] Implying that not all knowledge disappears when discursive thought ends.

[180] The fifth of the fifteen foundation letters of this novel is the *yud*. In many commentaries on the Hebrew alphabet, the shape of the *yud* is compared to that of the human brain.

[181] Reference to *seter*, the Hiding Place.

[182] Mostly, the *yud* as the first letter of the Tetragrammaton is thought of as unattainable, incomprehensible. Its round top, which makes up for most of its mass, is said to be located in the highest *sefirah Keter*, whereas its tail is in the second *sefirah Chokhmah*. Opinions as to the attainability of this sefirah are divided, but many texts suggest that one can reach this stage.

[183] When 'I' becomes 'there isn't' (see endnote 175), there is no entity left that implants the difference between the knower and the known. While this is true in general, Dov has now entered the world of the five (the *yud* is the fifth letter). Since the five times 'death' is where it all began (that is, this novel), death is stronger here, including 'Dov's death'. This is a different way of saying that his 'I' has become absent.

[184] He is in the realm of the five in general. The fifth letter *yud* turns the total of the first five letters at the foundation of the novel to 31. This ties in with the two pairs of the *abat* system that don't change when permuted (see end of endnote 169). Whereas the letters of these pairs, the *aleph* and the *lamed*, can be said to spell the godly name *El*, they can just as well be said to spell *al*, אל. Written in the same way as *El*, it nevertheless means

82

something completely different: 'not', 'do not' (used, for example, in the Hebrew rendering of the negative commandments). The Other is where what is known 'is not'. Also, 'the five is the essence', *heh etsem*, הא עצם, amounts to 206. This is the numerical value of the fifth plague: pestilence/plague, *dever*, דבר. Because the name of this plague actually means plague, it is natural to state that 'the five is the essence' (referring also to the five times that 'death' was used to gather the fifteen foundation letters of the novel). Having reached this self-affirming point in the progression of the ten plagues, the emphasis in the rest of the novel will shift slightly away from them.

[185] Reference to *vinafesh*, וינפש, of Exodus 31:17 (see endnote 28). The word has the same root as soul, *nefesh*, and has a numerical value of 446. This in turn refers to death, and to the state that Dov is in (see endnote 183).

[186] The *sefirah Chokhmah* (see endnote 182).

[187] Dov's withdrawal can be compared to inhaling. Creation however is withholding and giving. To enact this, Dov has to breathe out as well, thereby completing the circle.

[188] Remote pasture (as for example in Isaiah 5:17) is *dover*, דבר, with the same letters and value 206 as the fifth plague.

[189] '(He/she) said' is *davar*, דבר, also with the value 206.

[190] 'Dialogue' is *dibur*, דבור, from the root דבר, with the value 206.

[191] Reference to *male* of the *Bahir* that lead to the *abat* system (see endnote 169).

¹⁹² Reference to Job 5:5: 'Whose harvest the hungry eats up, and takes it even out of the thorns, and the robber swallows up their substance.' The word for whose is *asher*, 501, referring to the ten plagues (see endnote 80). 'The hungry' refers to the fourth plague of hunger. 'Eating' refers to the abat system and its permutation of *male* (see endnote 169), especially since here it is followed by *el*. Robber, *tsamim*, צמים, has the same root letters as *tsimtsum* (see endnote 178). The sentence in Hebrew has ten words, referring to the fifth, the *yud*, of the fifteen foundation letters that has the numerical value 10. The 'swallowing up' refers to withdrawal in general and to death in particular (via Isaiah 25:8: 'He will swallow up death in victory...'). The numerical value of all the last letters of the ten words of this verse amounts to 474. This is the value of the hidden *sefirah Da'at*, situated between *Chokhmah* and *Binah*. It is also a reference to equanimity and the Secret Garden (see also *To Kailash and Beyond*, chapter 23, *The extra letter*, and *The Absence of Direction*, chapter 6, *The soul of silence*). The total value of the last five words is the 206 of the fifth plague.

¹⁹³ The verb 'to bless' lay at the foundation of the permutation system *akhbi* (see endnote 143). The root of the word for blessing, *barakh*, through *akhbi* becomes *ain*, 'there isn't', denoting nothingness.

¹⁹⁴ In clean blood, *bedam naki*, בדם נקי, is 206 (of the fifth plague).

¹⁹⁵ Thorn is *dever* (for example in Psalm 91:3), דבר, with the value 206.

¹⁹⁶ *Dover* means both 'remote place' and 'remote pasture' (see endnote 188).

¹⁹⁷ 'That (there is) loveliness', *shechin*, שחין, is written exactly like the name of the sixth plague: boil. This signals the end of the dealings with the fifth plague.

[198] Paraphrasing 2 Samuel 22:16: 'And the channels of the sea appeared, the foundations of the world were discovered, at the rebuking of the Lord, at the blast of the breath of his nostrils.' This verse contains two of the five words for soul: *neshamah*, here translated as blast, and *ruach*, here translated as breath. The latter has the value of 214, which matches that of the first ten of the fifteen foundation letters of the novel. The tone is hereby set: the focus of this chapter will be on the ten. In the last chapter we had come to the fifth of the ten plagues, which implied a completion (see endnote 184). Now we move on from that fifth; the fifth of the fifteen foundation letters. We are thus left with the last ten letters of the fifteen gathered. The last four words of 2 Samuel 22:16 contain fifteen letters and are headed by the Tetragrammaton, emphasizing the connection between the fifteen foundation letters and this Name of Names. The final word of the verse is that for 'his nostrils', *afo*, אפו, and, since nose, af, amounts to 81, it can be read as 'his 81'. The number 81 is also found in the word for throne, *kise*, כסא. It is for this reason the subtitle ends in 'from his throne' instead of following the course of the original verse. Finally, there is a reference to a permutation system that will be dealt with only later in the chapter: the *abba* system (see endnote 210). Permuting af through this system, the outcome has the value of 10, reiterating the importance of that number. Exchanging this outcome for throne, the subtitle expresses the image of the foundations of the world having been laid bare by the blast of breath 'from his ten (*sefirot*)'.

[199] No-one is *af echad*. Through the first part of composite word, *af*, this name refers to the subtitle (see endnote 198). No-one also implies that God is One (see endnote 117).

[200] Reference to the title of chapter 2.

[201] Reference to Isaiah 25:8: 'He will swallow up death in victory; and the

Lord God will wipe away tears from off all faces; and the rebuke of his people shall he take away from off all the earth: for the Lord has spoken it.' As well as containing 'death' and hence connected to the fifteen foundation letters of the novel, the verse ends with the word *diber*, דבר. This has the value of 206, the same as the fifth plague that most of the references at the end of the preceding chapter were to (see endnotes 190, 192, 194-196).

[202] Reference to Genesis 12:1: 'Now the Lord had said unto Abram, Get out of your country, and from your kindred, and from your father's house, unto a land that I will show you.' This verse is mentioned in the Mishnah, Avot 5:3 (*avot*, literally 'fathers', is implied in the title of this chapter) as one of the ten (see endnote 198) verses telling about the ten trials with which God tried Abraham. The verse starts with 'and he said', *vayomer*, ויאמר, as do the ten verses that express the ten sayings with which the world was created. It ends with 'I will show you', *arekha*, אראך. This word amounts to 222, like the root of to bless, *barakh* (see endnotes 40, 115, 117, 143, 146, 193), implying the blessing of the letter *bet* (featuring in Genesis 12:1 and translated as house; see also endnotes 142-143). The last word of the verse can also spell 'I will lengthen', *a'arikh*, אאריך (see endnote 163), tying in with the notion of giving and withholding. Whereas the plagues can be seen as a gift (from God to Israel), the trials are the withholding.

[203] When permuting *tamar* through the *abat* system, the outcome is 26. This is the number of the Tetragrammaton, who is never absent.

[204] 'There was a famine' are the first words of Genesis 12:10, which is also mentioned in Avot 5:3 as one of the verses relating the ten trials of Abraham (see endnote 202. The two verses Genesis 12:1 and Genesis 12:10 are both mentioned in connection with the trial of having to move on). While the first word of Genesis 12:1 is *vayomer* (see endnote 202), that of Genesis 12:10 is *vayehi*, ויהי. Through yet another novel permutation system (the

afba system, see endnote 205) that will be discussed later, *vayehi* delivers the value 86. This is the value of the godly name *Elohim*, which, together with the first word of Genesis 12:1, gives us *vayomer Elohim*. These two words with the meaning 'and God said' are precisely those used at the start of the ten sayings with which the world was created.

[205] 'The presence of the five' refers to 'the five is the essence' (see endnote 184), and to the five times the word for death was used to obtain the fifteen foundation letters of this novel. By permutation with the *abat* system 'there are five', יש ה, gives the number 153. The ten of the fifteen foundation letters that have not been dealt with so far (the *bet, ayin, peh, lamed, aleph, bet, khaf, tav, vav*, and *mem*) can be rearranged to spell *mavet bekol aleph, peh, bet, ayin*, מות בכל אפבע. When taking those last four letters to denote a permutation system (they form two sequential pairs), this can be translated as: 'death (is found) in every (permutation of) *afba*.' These last four letters together amount to 153, and hence through *abat* confirm their place of origin: five times *mavet*, the word for death.

[206] Here am I, *hinneni*, הנני, is the last word of Genesis 22:1: 'And it came to pass after these things, that God did tempt Abraham, and said unto him, Abraham: and he said, Behold, here I am'. It is one of the ten verses relating Abraham's trials. This word *hinneni* amounts to 115, just as the word for 'he tempted', *nisah*, נסה, found in this same verse, does (Tamar's tempting undertone is a reference to this). Another 115 is found through the *afba* permutation of the word for five, *chamesh*, חמש. Finally, Genesis 22:1 contains all three words *vayomer, Elohim*, and *vayehi* in that sequence in five of the ten verses that make up the ten sayings with which the world was created (see endnote 204).

[207] Reference to Deuteronomy 9:22: 'And at Taberah, and at Massah, and at Kibrothhattaavah, you provoked the Lord to wrath.' The verse is one of

the ten named in Avot 5:3 as pertaining to the ten trials of the fathers. The third place mentioned in this verse, Kibrothhattaavah, can be divided into *kibroth* and *ha-ta'avah*. The last word means desire.

208 'The Other' is *ha'acher*, האחר, and amounts to 214. This is also the value of the sixth generation when counting from Adam: Yered. Yered was the father (see title of the chapter) of Chenokh who, one can say, was taken in by the Other: 'And Chenokh walked with God: and he was not; for God took him'(Gen. 5:24). Acher is also the second word of Genesis 22:1 (see endnote 206). It follows upon *vayehi*, and precedes *hadevarim ha'eleh*, 'these things'. The word for thing here is *davar*, of the same root as *dibur*, speech (see endnote 190), and thereby refers to the (ten) sayings with which the world was created.

209 Reference to Tamar: *tamar* through *akhbi* becomes *lashon*, tongue.

210 Reference to Genesis 17:23: 'And Abraham took Ishmael his son, and all that were born in his house, and all that were bought with his money, every male among the men of Abraham's house; and circumcised the flesh of their foreskin in the selfsame day, as God had said unto him.' It is one of the verses mentioned in Avot 5:3 as reflecting Abraham's ten trials. When permuting Ishmael with the *abat* system ('all that were born in his house' refers to this system that is based upon the *bet*, the house), the outcome is 112. This equals the value of the *abat* of *mavet*, death. However, this verse takes us further than a mere reiteration of the importance of death. The root of the word for circumcision that is mentioned in Genesis 17:23 is *mul*, מול. When taking the *vav*, literally the hook, as the permuting entity, this word offers us a pair, *mem* and *lamed*, of a new permutation system. When taking the *mem* as being part of the row that goes up (*mem* followed by the *nun*, *samekh*, etc.), and the *lamed* as part of the row that goes down (*lamed* followed by the *khaf*, *yud*, etc.), a system crystallizes in which the first two

pairs are *aleph-bet* and *bet-aleph*. When reading these four letters in that sequence, we get *abba*, father. This system explicitly refers to the title of this chapter, and to *avot*, the fathers.

²¹¹ Reference to *tsimtsum* (see endnote 178).

²¹² A form of Shiva, a Hindu deity, who is half male, half female.

²¹³ The fifteen letters that are the foundation of this novel; they are the result of a special use of the word for death, *mavet*, מות (see *Prologue*).

²¹⁴ Although No-one has 'crossed over to the other side', he doesn't know this (see also 'to know is to no know' in *To Kailash and Beyond*, chapter 10: *The fruit of the palm tree*). Instead, he thinks that he might be on the wrong path, apparently staring himself blind on Death and ignoring the fact that true life is what his quest is about. Tamar's last remark was meant to steer him away from these discursive thoughts. The house mentioned by her refers to permutation systems in general and the *abat* system in particular. This is the last system that is wholly included in the mystical story. According to Tamar, No-one has been revived, has spiritually grown, through the use of permutation systems: he is as if reborn. However, just like permutation systems consist of two rows; the world, though founded on simplicity, was created in duality; withdrawing precedes giving; and after breathing in, one always breathes out; life and death are interconnected. This is implied in the system that was born from Genesis 17:23: the *abba* system. The One (*aleph*) retreats for the two (*bet*) to found creation, but creation (*bet*) always leads back to the One (*aleph*; see also the word for 'he created', *bara*, ברא, whose first letter *bet* leads to its last letter *aleph*): *abba*. The fact that this system, mentioned as an additional remark in endnote 198, is not used to permutate, but remains withdrawn (though tempting, much like the life beyond the cracks in the screen of reality is withdrawn and tempts No-

one), means that this part of the story takes place within it. No-one is inside the realm of *abba*, the Father, when he is visited by discursive thought. The notion of a fixed and final enlightenment at the end of the religious path is hereby disputed. The argument is that there is no temporal ending point within spirituality; this is merely the assimilation of religious concepts by dual thought. In reality, enlightenment is not a static state, but one that is very much alive and moving. In short, No-one is being tempted by his own thought-system.

215 'The beginning of truth' refers to the *abat* system, whose first pair is twice the *aleph*. This letter is literally the beginning of the word for truth: *emet*, אמת. Taking the two *alephs* as the two beginning letters of the first and last words of the name *Ehuyeh asher Ehuyeh* (a beginning in its own right, being the godly name associated with *Keter*, the first *sefirah*), they can each be said to refer to the 21 (*Ehuyeh* equals 21). Squared, 21 becomes the 441 of *emet* (see endnote 83). 'The beginning' is also a reference to the first word of the Torah: *bereshit*, בראשית. This word can be rearranged to spell 'in the fear of the *shin*', ש ביראת. The shin amounts to 300, which is the total value of the *atbash* equivalent of the Tetragrammaton. For the connection between 'the fear of God' and 'the Seeing of God', see *To Kailash and Beyond*, chapter 6, *The blessing of the king*.

216 If 'the fear of God' is the beginning of truth, it can be deduced that 'the rest of truth' is found in what follows 'the fear of God'. In No-one's spiritual development, fear is always overcome, which could be phrased as 'the death of fear'. If death is what follows fear, then death should also be 'the rest of truth'. When putting the 'beginning of truth', the *aleph*, aside, one is left with the letters *mem* and *tav*. Together they spell 'he died', *met*, מת. It turns out that death is indeed 'the rest of truth': the argument has come full circle.

²¹⁷ When truth is understood to be merely a subjective theory, then it can be seen as externally imposed. The same can be said of any person's personal spiritual path. When both truth and a person's spiritual path are perceived in this way, then the one theory will indeed come to negate the other. However, in this novel, truth is seen as That-Which-Is, containing all of life. A personal path is something that is received as opposed to imposed, and tells a person what the key elements for personal development are. Seen in this way, the path cannot possibly negate the truth, since it is part of it.

²¹⁸ Again the parable of breathing in and out is relevant (see endnote 214). Life is the giving force, whereas the path can be seen as the withholding force.

²¹⁹ No-one is still experiencing discursive thought. The melancholy refers to the pull of the life behind the cracks in reality.

²²⁰ As long as one makes space for God, the entity that is making the space is still blocking God out.

²²¹ Reference to Psalm 106:9: 'He rebuked the Red Sea also, and it was dried up: so he led them through the depths, as through the wilderness.' The verse's relevance comes from the fact that Psalm 106:7 is mentioned in Avot 5:3 as one of those relating the ten trials of the fathers. The reference is to No-one whose discursive thoughts are his own trial at the moment. 'In the depths' of Psalm 106:9 is written as *bathomot*, בתהמות. When inserting a space in this word after the second letter, we get *bet ha-mavet*, בת המות, meaning 'the house of death'. The 'wilderness', *midbar*, in the same verse refers to *tohu* and *bohu*, but, with its root being *davar*, also to the 206 of the fifth (plague).

²²² The fact that No-one listened to, but did not identify with, his discursive

thoughts means that he passed the trial. It is also a reference to Psalm 106:7 (see endnote 221): 'Our fathers did not understand your wonders in Egypt; they did not remember the multitude of your mercies; but they provoked him at the sea, even at the Red Sea.' The last word of this verse is *suf*, סוף, part of the name the Red Sea: *yam suf*. This refers to *Ain Sof*, אין סוף. The further relevance of this verse lies in the fact that it contains 'fathers' (referring to the title of this chapter and Avot), and 'wonders', *nifla'ot*. This last word refers to the opening line of *Sefer Yetsirah*, where 'the thirty-two paths of wonderful wisdom' are mentioned.

[223] In order to draw such a conclusion, No-one would have had to identify with his name, which would have entailed more discursive thought.

[224] Via the word for 'they provoked' from Psalm 106:7. The word *tamar*, literally meaning 'date palm', was instrumental in discovering the *akhbal* system (see *To Kailash and Beyond*, chapter 10, *The fruit of the palm tree*). In that process, the word used for 'permutation' was *tmurah*, of the same root as *tamar*. In the same chapter of *To Kailash and Beyond*, Exodus 23:21 is used to connect the word for 'to provoke' with *tamar*. Instead of reading 'and do not provoke him', *al tamar bo*, אל תמר בו, this verse is interpreted as 'the God of *tamar* is in him'. Also, the word for melancholy, which No-one thought he had to conquer, is of the same root as that for 'to provoke'.

[225] From the word for 'and they provoked', *vayamru*, וימרו, in Psalm 106:7, the step is made to the word for 'he will change it', *yemirenu*, ימירנו, in Leviticus 27:33 (which also contains the word *tmurah*, see endnote 224): 'He shall not search whether it be good or bad, neither shall he change it: and if he change it at all, then both it and the change thereof shall be holy; it shall not be redeemed.'

[226] Reference to the beginning of this paragraph (see page 105).

[227] Reference to Avot 5:6, where ten things are listed that were created on the eve of the Shabbat, in the twilight. This *mishnah* contains a reference to Ecclesiastes 1:9: '...there is nothing new under the sun.' This implies that what is new, can only come about in the twilight.

[228] Reference to the ten things that were created in the twilight (see endnote 227). One of them is 'the mouth of the earth' as mentioned in Numbers 16:32: 'And the earth opened her mouth, and swallowed them up, and their houses, and all the men that appertained unto Korah, and all their goods.' The word house in this verse also refers to the *abat* permutation system (see endnote 210). 'Their houses', *batehem*, בתיהם, can also mean 'their bets', referring to the first verses of the *Bahir* in which the bet takes a central place (see endnotes 102, 137, 146, and 169). Finally, the 'swallowing up' of this verse refers to that of Isaiah 25:8 (see endnote 192).

[229] Reiterating the fact that No-one is inside the *abba* system and does not use it to permute (see endnote 214).

[230] The (mouth of the) well is another of the things created in the twilight, according to Numbers 21:16: 'And from there they went to Beer: that is the well whereof the Lord spoke unto Moses, Gather the people together, and I will give them water.' The well, *habe'er*, הבאר, also spells *bara heh*, ברא ה, meaning 'he created five'. This refers to the five times that death was used as the foundation of this novel. However, both words also amount to 208, which is the numerical value of the locusts that form the eighth plague: *arbeh*, ארבה. After the fifth plague, we stopped dealing with the plagues one by one in order of occurrence. The sixth was only alluded to once (see endnote 197). The seventh, hail, is skipped, since it has the same letters and numerical value as the fifth (*barad*, ברד), so now we have reached the eighth plague. The number 208 is significant since it is the outcome of the *afba* permutation of *mavet becol* (see endnote 205). The last ten letters of

93

the fifteen foundation letters thereby spelled the recommendation of this permutation themselves: '(permute the words) *mavet becol* (with the) *afba* (system).' This is only a confirmation of the synchronicity of the various story lines, No-one himself does not perform this permutation. The reason why the well is called that 'of nothingness' is because of the word for gather, *esof*, in Numbers 21:16. *Esof*, אסף, also spells 'zero/nothing', *efes*, אפס. This refers to *Ain Sof*, the realm beyond the *sefirot*. In the mystical union with the godhead, this is what one unites with: the Nothingness beyond all theories and paths.

[231] Reference to the dew with which the dead will be revived (see endnote 94).

[232] The rainbow is another of the ten things that according to Avot 5:6 were created in the twilight.

[233] Reference to Exodus 16:14: 'And when the dew that lay was gone up, behold, upon the face of the wilderness there lay a small round thing, as small as the hoar frost on the ground.' This verse is mentioned in Avot 5:6 where the ten things created at twilight are enumerated. In this case the thing created is the manna, which is named in Exodus 16:15.

[234] The word for 'round thing' is *mechuspas*, מחספס, the last four letters of which amount to 208 (see endnote 230). In this case it is unclear if this word is a foreign root of four letters, or a Hebrew root, since this word only appears once in the Torah, and there are no other passages to compare its meaning.

[235] This is the direct translation of the root חספס: to crackle.

[236] Reference to the word for 'he will laugh', *yitschak*, יצחק. This is also the name of Isaac in Hebrew. It amounts to 208 (see endnote 230).

[237] Reference to Exodus 16:31: 'And the house of Israel called the name thereof manna: and it was like coriander seed, white; and the taste of it was like wafers made with honey.' The word for manna used here is *man*, מן. It is compared to coriander, *gad*, גד. Taking the four letters of these two words as part of a permutation system, the *mem* and the *nun* of *man* belong to one row, and the *gimmel* and the *dalet* of *gad* to the other. The permutation system that thus crystallizes, has two rows running in the same direction (like the *akhbal* system; see *To Kailash and Beyond*, chapter 10, *The fruit of the palm tree*). Its first two pairs are *aleph-mem* and *bet-nun*, and it is therefore called the *amban* system. Just as the esoteric *abba* system remains untouched by No-one, so too does this system. It stands second to the *abba* system in importance; its first two pairs being the words for mother and son respectively, while *abba* means father.

[238] Tamar reminds him of the fact that the sons and daughters of the houses, being the results of the permutation systems, are negated (see endnote 228). Implied here are the *abba* and *amban* systems that are present, but remain untouched. Judges 11:34 ('And Jephthah came to Mizpeh unto his house, and, behold, his daughter came out to meet him with timbrels and with dances: and she was his only child; beside her he had neither son nor daughter') furthermore contains the word *yechidah*, יחידה, 'beside her', which is also the fourth name for soul (there are five names, the first three, *nefesh*, *ruach*, and *neshamah*, have already been dealt with in the previous chapters, the fifth name, *chayah*, will be dealt with in the fifth chapter).

[239] Here Tamar is a reference to *tmurah*, permutation (see endnote 224).

²⁴⁰ Reference to Genesis 30:37: 'And Jacob took him rods of green poplar, and of the hazel and chestnut tree; and peeled white strips in them, and made the white appear which was in the rods.' The word for 'made appear', *machshof*, מחשף, of this verse comes from the root that, according to some commentaries on Exodus 16:14 (see endnote 233), the word for manna, *mechuspas* is derived from.

²⁴¹ The fig tree refers to the Garden of Eden. Also reference to Joel 1:7: 'He has laid my vine waste, and barked my fig tree: he has made it clean bare, and cast it away; the branches thereof are made white.' The 'making bare' of this verse is from the same linguistic root as 'to make appear' (see endnote 240). In addition, the word for fig is *tu'enah*, תאנה, which has the same value 456 as 'my death', *maveti*, מותי.

²⁴² Reference to Isaiah 52:10: 'The Lord hath made bare his holy arm in the eyes of all the nations; and all the ends of the earth shall see the salvation of our God.' The verse contains the word for 'making bare' (see endnote 241). However, with the mention of the right arm, the verse also contains a reference to a hymn that starts with the words 'God whose mighty (right) hand makes nations free'. The relevance of this hymn lies in the fact that it is ascribed to the same person who the *Bahir* is ascribed to: rav. Nehuniah ben haKana, a Talmudic sage from the first century AD. This hymn is of further importance to the novel because it is connected with the forty-two lettered name of God. The hymn contains forty-two words, and in some mystical texts the first letters of these words, permuted with various systems, are related to the letters of the forty-two lettered name.

²⁴³ Reference to Psalm 29:9: 'The voice of the Lord makes the hinds to calve, and discovers the forests: and in his temple doth every one speak of his glory.' The word for 'to discover' comes from the same root as 'made appear' (see endnote 240). The fact that they are the forests of speech refers

96

to *davar*, which is the root of the word for saying (reference to the ten sayings with which the world was created), and has the value 206 of the fifth plague.

[244] 'To hew' comes from the root *chakak*, חקק, which has the value 208 (see endnote 230), and is mentioned in the first sentence of *Sefer Yetsirah*.

[245] 'Release' also features in the hymn's first sentence: 'God whose mighty hand makes nations free, release all captives, hear our humble plea' (see endnote 242).

[246] In general, sparks that need to be released refer to the theory of Isaac Luria (see endnote 178). He held that during the cosmic process a disaster occurred in which the vessels that were intended to hold the divine light broke because they couldn't contain this light. The sparks of these lights supposedly fell into the lower worlds, and were kept captive there by the forces of *Geburah*. The freeing of these sparks implies restoration, *tikkun*. In particular the reference is to melancholy, recently observed by No-one without identifying with it, thereby releasing its sparks.

[247] Reference to the various forms supposed to be found in the root of the word for manna, *mechuspas* (see endnote 234): to make bare, to discover, to uncover.

[248] When spelling the word for forests, *ya'arot*, in its concise form יערת, it amounts to 680. When adding the letter *bet* to denote the fact that No-one is going into them, the total value is 682. This is the total numerical value of the fifteen foundation letters of this novel. It also matches the value of the name for Hebrew, *ivrit*, עברית. Hence the forests of speech.

[249] The word for wonder is *ot*, אות, just like the word for letter. They only

differ in their plural forms, where wonders becomes *otot*, אותות, and letters *oti'ot*, אותיות.

[250] Reference to 'release all captives' from the first sentence of the hymn (see endnote 245).

[251] Rain is water, *mayim*, מים, which has the same numerical value as manna, *man*: 90. It is also connected to dew, with which the dead will be revived (see Isaiah 26:19). Finally it is *geshem*, גשם, which has the value 343, matching that of *vayomer Elohim* (see endnote 204), and thus referring to the ten sayings of God and the forests of speech.

[252] Youngster is *na'ar*, נער, which is the *afba* equivalent of *davar*, the root behind *dibur*, speech.

[253] Reference to the Torah: *torah* can also mean instruction.

[254] Reference to the kabbalistic idea of drawing down the forces of the letters of high into the letters of this world. The trees are seen as the *sefirot* that channel them; the *sefirot* are also often depicted as a tree.

[255] Tamar didn't join him since 682 minus the 640 of *tamar* amounts to 42; the hymn and its affiliations have revived the importance of the forty-two lettered name. 'He is alone'/ 'on his own' is *levado*, לבדו, also 42. Plurality is *riboei*, רבוי, which shares its 228 with the last plague: 'the first born', *bekhor*, בכור. The one but last plague, that of darkness, is implied in the forests of speech through which no sunlight penetrates. The sentence also refers to *yechid*, unique, which in turn refers to *yechidah*, the fourth name of the soul (see endnote 238).

[256] Reference to the second sentence of the hymn (see endnote 242): 'Accept this plaintive song we offer you to praise and glorify your name.'

[257] Reference to Psalm 89:9 (8): 'O Lord God of hosts, who is a strong Lord like you? Or to your faithfulness round about you?' The first three words of this verse, translated as 'O Lord God of hosts', contain three godly names, the last one of which is *Tsevaot* (see endnotes 36, 46, and 56). It is by these three names that God is addressed with the question: 'Who is like you?' The three names amount to 571, which is also the value of 'I will get stuck', *etka*, אתקע. This psalm furthermore contains the word *chasin*, which also features in the fifth sentence of the hymn and there is translated as pure: 'Holy and pure, with all of your mercy, shepherd your flock.'

[258] Reference to the last, seventh, sentence of the hymn: 'Accept our supplication and hear our cries, knower of deep mysteries.'

[259] Reference to the second sentence of the hymn: 'Accept this plaintive song we offer you to praise and glorify your name.' The word that is translated as 'to exalt/to praise' is from the same root as 'safety'.

[260] Reference to Proverbs 18:10: 'The name of the Lord is a strong tower: the righteous run into it, and are safe.' The last word of this verse is of the same root as 'to exalt/to praise' (see endnote 259).

[261] Reference to the hymn of endnote 242 in general.

[262] Reference to Psalm 44:22 (21): 'Shall not God search this out? For he knows the secrets of the heart.' The 'knower of (deep) mysteries' of the last sentence of the hymn (see endnote 258), is a paraphrase of 'he knows the secrets'.

[263] Reference to the fifth sentence of the hymn: 'Holy and pure, with all of your mercy shepherd your flock.'

[264] The first letters of the words for body, soul, and essence, *guf*, *neshamah*, and *etsem*, עצם, נשמה, גוף, are *gimmel*, *nun*, *ayin*. Together they form the first three letters of the five lettered *gan eden*, גן עדן, the Garden of Eden.

[265] The root of the word for 'to know' starts with a *dalet*, the fourth letter of the five making *gan eden*, the Garden of Eden. Knowledge, *da'at*, contains the same letters as 'flock' of the fifth sentence of the hymn (see endnote 263).

[266] The idea being that in order to overcome discursive thought, one does not judge it. One watches the thoughts without interference (including identification) to let them blossom fully. Only thus can one see them clearly and, when their irrelevance is completely understood, let them go.

[267] This process of entering the soul of the beast is the 'uncovering' No-one was sensing (see endnote 247). It implies the last of the five letters that makes up *gan eden*, the Garden of Eden, the *nun*. Not overtly present in its normal shape, the *nun*, 50, is here referred to by the two letters *mem* and *yud*, that together also amount to 50. They are found in Psalm 89:9 (8) (see endnote 257) where, following the three holy names the verse opens with, it is written 'who is like you', *me kamokha*, מי כמוך. Since *kamokha* amounts to 86 of *Elohim*, when taking me as a holy name as well (in some kabbalistic texts this word is looked upon as the name of an angel who holds the power to annul what God has done [see also *The Absence of Direction*, chapter 5, *The advent of strength*]), this verse opens with five holy names, each represented by one of the five letters of *gan eden*. Permuting me with the *afba* system, the outcome is the two letters *heh* and *chet*. Together with the *mem* and the *yud* of *me*, they form the word *mechayeh*, מחיה. When read as a verb, this means

'he/she/it revives', referring to the dew of the well (see endnote 231), and to mystical death and life in general: by mystically dying to the past every moment, one is as if reborn every moment as well. When reading *mechayeh*, מחיה, as a noun with a pronoun, it means 'from the beast'. The five letters of *gan eden*, the Secret Garden, have now been completed. Together these five letters amount to 177, which refers to the hymn of rav. HaKana (see endnote 242): the hymn contains 7 sentences and 170 letters: 7+170=177. The number 177 is also found as the total of the three godly names *yud heh vav heh*, *Elohim*, and *Adonai*. The five is hence fulfilled on many levels. The beast itself refers to the book of Ezekiel where the vision of the beast is described. It thereby also refers to *ma'aseh merkabah*, מעשה מרכבה, which amounts to 682 (see endnote 35).

[268] The relevance of Ezekiel 28:6 lies in the fact that the three godly names *yud heh vav heh*, *Elohim*, and *Adonai* feature in it (see endnote 267). Their combined value is 177, like that of *gan eden*, the Garden of Eden.

[269] Reference to 2 Samuel 7:22: 'Wherefore you are great, O Lord God: for there is none like you, neither is there any God beside you, according to all that we have heard with our ears.' Also in this verse the three godly names *yud heh vav heh*, *Elohim*, and *Adonai* appear (see endnote 268). The verse furthermore contains the phrase *me kamokha* (see endnote 267). The interchanging of 'ears' with 'hearts' is a reference to the subtitle of this chapter.

[270] Identification with discursive, opinionated thought is regarded as the main characteristic of the result of the influence of the beast.

[271] 'Living soul' is *nefesh chayah* (see endnotes 7, 64, and 69); *chayah* is the fifth and highest name for soul.

[272] Reference to *Sefer Yetsirah* (see endnote 109).

[273] Reference to *To Kailash and Beyond* in its entirety.

[274] Reference to the five souls a person has (see endnote 238).

[275] Reference to *Ain Sof* (see endnotes 47, 148, 222, and 230).

[276] 'Male and female' is *zakhar venekevah* and amounts to 390 (see endnote 19).

[277] Reference to Ezekiel 1:5: 'Also out of the midst thereof came the likeness of four living creatures. And this was their appearance; they had the likeness of a man.'

[278] Reference to Genesis 12:5: '...and the souls that they had made in Charan...' The word for soul here is *nefesh*, the first and lowest of the five souls. In Charan, *becharan*, בחרן, amounts to 260, referring to the presence of the Tetragrammaton in each of the ten *sefirot* (see also *The Absence of Direction*, chapter 1, *The birth of sobriety*).

[279] Reference to Deuteronomy 34:1-4 where Moses is shown the promised land but is not allowed to enter it.

[280] The not leaving any traces denotes a state of mind where one dies to the past continually.

[281] Reference to Deuteronomy 34:1: 'And Moses went up from the plains of Moab unto the mountain of Nebo, to the top of Pisgah, that is over against Jericho. And the Lord showed him all the land of Gilead, unto Dan.' It is also a reference to the names of the five souls. Their combined afba value

is 668, which is 14 short of the total 682 of the fifteen foundation letters. The number 14 spells *yad*, יד, which through *afba* becomes *chen*, חן. Chen, as well as meaning grace, and being the *afba* rendering of *chayah*, the fifth soul, also shares its number 58 with (Mount) Nebo. (So does 'the Garden', *hagan*, הגן).

282 Reference to Deuteronomy 34:3: 'And the south, and the plain of the valley of Jericho, the city of palm trees, unto Zoar.' Also a reference to Tamar and the discovery of the *akhbal* system (see *To Kailash and Beyond*, chapter 10, *The fruit of the palm tree*).

283 Reference to Ezekiel 14:5: 'If I cause noisome beasts to pass through the land, and they spoil it, so that it be desolate, that no man may pass through because of the beasts.' The word for beast is the same as the name of the highest soul: *chayah*. Although No-one is in a highly developed spiritual state, not all of his five souls are completely purified, completely devoid from opinionated thought. This is why he cannot enter Charan, and why he sees the beasts at all. In the realm of the highest soul, the unknown is so pure and powerful that to the known (opinionated thought on all possible levels) it translates as its worst fear. In response to this fear, thought clothes the unknown with known images, thereby pulling it into the known. In this case the unknown is personified as a terrifying beast. Inherent to the holding on to the conditioned way of thinking is the division of That-Which-Is. This is here represented by 'desolate', a reference to the division of *tohu* and *bohu*, formless and void (see endnote 31).

284 Reference to Deuteronomy 34:5: 'So Moses the servant of the Lord died there in the land of Moab, according to the word of the Lord.' 'According to the word' is *al pi*, על פי, which can also be read as 'by the mouth'. Mystical commentaries state that this refers to mystical death by godly kiss. The reading 'according to the word' also implies some kind of command, and

as such, 'word' can be exchanged for 'statutes'. In that latter case this refers to Ezekiel 18:9: 'Has walked in my statutes, and has kept my judgments, to deal truly; he is just, he shall surely live, says the Lord God.' This verse contains the word *chayah*. The three words preceding *chayah* in Hebrew can also be read as '(it is the) truth that the righteous is'. The Hebrew words that in the verse have been translated as 'truly; he is just', *emet tsadik*, אמת צדיק, are the first and second of these three words (the third being *hu*, he is) preceding and indicating the meanings held by *chayah*. Together these two words amount to 645. Deducting this from the total 682 of the fifteen foundation letters, one gets 37. This is the value of the heart, *halev*, הלב, explaining why No-one 'speaks his heart'. It is also the value of *yechidah*, יחידה, the name of the fourth soul. Deducting 645 from 651 (the number of the last ten of the fifteen foundation letters), one is left with 6, the number of the letter *vav*. Inserting this letter into *emet tsadik*, אמת צדיק, it can read *amut tsadik*, אמות צדיק, 'I, the righteous, will die'.

[285] Reference to Deuteronomy 34:6: 'And he buried him in a valley in the land of Moab, over against Bethpeor: but no man knows of his sepulcher unto this day.' The words 'over against Bethpeor' in Hebrew are *mul beit peor*, מול בית פעור, the first two of which mean 'opposite the house'. The *beit* can be taken as a reference to the *abat* system, whose second pair also spells house, and the *mul* as a reference to the *abba* system, that was discovered through that word (see endnote 210). However, the *atbash* system also features strongly through the word for sepulcher, *kever*, קבר. This word has the numerical value of 302, which is also the value of 'in the 300', *be-300*. This refers to the *atbash* equivalent of the Tetragrammaton, which amounts to 300 (a more hidden reference is to Genesis 1:2 where 'the spirit of God, *ruach Elohim*, רוח אלהים, also amounts to 300; hence it points to the next name for soul). Thus there are references to three permutation systems in this verse, explaining the use of 'trinity'. The trinity however also refers to

what has yet to be dealt with: the first three letters of the first name *Ehuyeh*, and the first three letters of the fifteen foundation letters.

[286] The root of the word *peor* from Deuteronomy 34:6 (see endnote 285) through *atbash* has the value of 16, matching that of the first three letters of the first name *Ehuyeh*, and the first three letters of the fifteen foundation letters.

[287] The number of the beast, according to Revelation 13:18, is 666. When deducting that from the 682 of the fifteen foundation letters, one is left with 16 (see endnote 286).

[288] Reference to the Jewish mystical trend of *Merkabah*. Its literary remains are traceable over a period of almost a thousand years, from the first century BC to the tenth AD. The mystics of this group called themselves 'the descenders to the *Merkabah*'. The *merkabah* itself denotes the esoteric doctrine of creation, which has the book of Ezekiel as its source.

[289] 'Charan' through *afba* becomes 214, the number of the second soul, *ruach*, רוח. Its direct permutation is *yered*, the name of the father of Chenokh who did not die by the kiss of God or anything as intimate as that. He was simply 'taken away' (see endnote 117). The conciseness of the description of Chenokh's death is taken to refer to the absence of hope of reward etc. that could be read into the more overtly intimate godly kiss.

[290] The lake is the same one mentioned at the beginning of chapter 1. The five refers to the five souls and the five times the word for death was used to obtain the fifteen foundation letters. The fifth day refers to Ezekiel 1:2: 'In the fifth day of the month, which was the fifth year of king Jehoiachin's captivity.'

²⁹¹ Reference to Ezekiel 1:4: 'And I looked, and, behold, a whirlwind came out of the north..' The word for wind here is *ruach*, רוח, referring to the second soul.

²⁹² Reference to the second soul, *ruach*; 'to breathe' comes from the same root as the third name for soul: *neshamah*.

²⁹³ Reference to Isaiah 57:16: 'For I will not contend for ever, neither will I be always wroth: for the spirit should fail before me, and the souls which I have made.' 'The spirit .. before me' is *ruach lefanai*, now the head wind that meets the protagonist. Isaiah 57:16 hence contains the word *ruach*, the second soul, but also *neshamah* (here in plural: 'the souls which I have made'), the third soul. Finally, the 'I have made' refers to the first soul, *nefesh*, about which it is said in Genesis 12:5 that it was made in Charan. The verse brings the discussion to the fourth level of the soul.

²⁹⁴ Both the word for contest, *rivah*, ריבה, and the word for victory, *netsach*, נצח, appear in Isaiah 57:16. The former is represented in the verb *lehariv*, להריב, 'to contend'. The latter appears as the Hebrew conjunction 'always', *lenetsach*, לנצח.

²⁹⁵ Meditation teaches about the concept of fear and how it reigns over our lives as the source of discursive thought. The rise above it implies the capacity to not identify with one's thoughts. The verb 'to fail' also appears in Isaiah 57:16 (see endnote 293).

²⁹⁶ Reference to Ezekiel 18:17: 'That has taken off his hand from the poor..' This verse also contains the word *chayah*. The poor refers to those who cannot rise above failure and remain stuck in the framework of opposites like spiritual success and failure. The hand also refers to grace (see endnote 281).

[297] Reference to Ezekiel 18:17 (see endnote 296), and to *The Absence of Direction*. The cover of that novel depicts this scene, and it is dealt with in its chapter 8, *Human skull cups*.

[298] Reference to the end of Ezekiel 18:17: '…he shall not die for the iniquity of his father, he shall surely live.' The mention of father refers to the *abba* system, the first two pairs of which make up this word. Permuting *chayah*, the word that follows on from 'his father', according to this system, one gets *peser*, פסר, the letters of which also spell *sefer*, ספר, book.

[299] Reference to Ezekiel 18:19: 'Yet say you, Why? does not the son bear the iniquity of the father? When the son has done that which is lawful and right, and has kept all my statutes, and has done them, he shall surely live.' This verse contains the word *chayah*. One can take its mention of the son as a reference to the *amban* system, because this system's second pair spells *ben*, son. Permuting the word for good, *tov*, by means of the *amban* system, one gets the value 440. This spells the word *tam*, תם, meaning innocent, simple.

[300] Reference to Ezekiel 18:19 (see endnote 299). The words for 'lawful and right' are *mishpat utsdakah*, משפט וצדקה, and amount to 634. Deducting this value from the 651 of the last ten of the fifteen foundation letters, one gets 17. This is the value of 'good', *tov*, טוב (see endnote 299), hence the 'goodness' of the law. 'Law' is a reference to the Torah, which translates as that. The goodness and justness mentioned refer to the layer that the protagonist is now experiencing: the layer of understanding where equanimity rules and the discursive quality of words becomes meaningless. Here even the letters become meaningless; they are taken for what they are and not clothed with connotations, cognomen, or the like. The last reference points in this direction as well. It is connected to the word good as it appears in Genesis 1:31: 'And God saw everything that he had made, and, behold, it was very

good…' According to some commentaries, the reason why in this verse, unlike in the preceding ones that also end with 'and God saw it was good' (Genesis 1:10, 12, 18, 21, and 25) the word 'very' is used because it points to death. This is based on the fact that the word for death, *mavet*, מות, only differs from that for very, *me'od*, מאד, by one letter. Hence the implication is that death is good, here interpreted as the goodness of the death of the discursive thought system. The result of this good death is that the protagonist is capable of penetrating the deeper layers of the text.

[301] The last two sentences paraphrase Daniel 7:11: 'I beheld then because of the voice of the pompous words which the horn spoke: I beheld even till the beast was slain, and his body destroyed, and given to the burning flame.' The beast that is slain here is the discursive thought system, which ascribed meaning to the letters. The letters now disintegrate and lose their material quality. This is expressed by the word *geshem*, which also means rain and shares its numerical with *vayomer Elohim* (see endnotes 204, 252). The fact that the underlying flames emit the sounds and later destroy them refers to the statement of *Sefer Yetsirah* 1:6 that the end is embedded in the beginning. This circular quality is firstly confirmed by the fact that the last three letters of the fifteen foundation letters (their end) spell *mavet*, death, while they, the foundation letters, they were revealed by means of that word as well (their beginning). Secondly this is confirmed by those last three letters appearing in reversed order: the last letter of *mavet* appears first, and the first last.

[302] Although no overt mention is made of the succession of the various layers of the soul, this has become clear in the endnotes. In the preceding paragraphs the first three layers *nefesh*, *ruach*, and *neshamah* have taken the stage, now it is the turn of the fourth: *yechidah*. The sentence paraphrases the beginning of Daniel 7:19: 'Then I would know the truth of the fourth beast, which was diverse from all the others…'

[303] Reference to the beginning of Daniel 7:14: 'And there was given him dominion, and glory, and a kingdom, that all people, nations, and languages, should serve him...' Also a more hidden reference to the three 'books', three layers of reality that are mentioned in *Sefer Yetsirah* 1:1.

[304] Reference to Daniel 7:28: '.. As for me Daniel, my cogitations much troubled me, and my countenance changed in me..'

[305] Reference to Daniel 7:19: 'Then I would know the truth of the fourth beast, which was diverse from all the others, exceeding dreadful, whose teeth were of iron, and his nails of brass; which devoured, broke in pieces, and stamped the residue with his feet.'

[306] The urge described is that of the thought system we called 'I'. The I's conditioning is to have control over life in general, and to identify with chosen occurrences in particular. An echo of this tendency is found in the responses to more intricate spiritual insights where one feels the need to identify oneself with experiences that one thinks exemplify a certain valuable lesson or stage.

[307] Reference to Daniel 7:25: 'And he shall speak great words against the most High, and shall wear out the saints of the most High, and think to change times and laws...' Also refers to the falling apart of the strongholds of discursive thought.

[308] All along the Secret Soul Garden, the Hidden Garden, has referred to the Garden of Eden. This case is no different, with an additional reference to Daniel 7:25 which contains three different renderings of the word *eden*. Three renderings points to the three books of *Sefer Yetsirah* (see endnote 303). Furthermore, 'Hiding Place' is *seter*, 660. Deducted from the 682 of the fifteen foundation letters, one is left with 22. This refers to the twenty-

two letters of the Hebrew alphabet, and to the fact that the protagonist is now at their numerical level of reality.

[309] Reference to Daniel 7:24: 'And the ten horns out of this kingdom are ten kings that shall arise: and another shall rise after them; and he shall be diverse from the first, and he shall subdue three kings.' The three refers to the three books of *Sefer Yetsirah*, the three mother letters as mentioned there (*Sefer Yetsirah* 3:1-9), and the first three layers of the soul.

[310] Now the protagonist enters the level of the fourth soul called *yechidah*, יחידה. The opening refers to Judges 11:34: 'And Jephthah came to Mizpeh unto his house, and, behold, his daughter came out to meet him with timbrels and with dances: and she was his only child; beside her he had neither son nor daughter.' The name Jephthah can also be read as a verb and then means 'he will open', *yiftach*, יפתח. This is the only verse in the Tenakh that contains the word *yechidah*, although not in the sense of 'soul': here it means 'only child'.

[311] The word *yiftach* of Judges 11:34 (see endnote 310) has the numerical value of 498. The word for 'in(to) the kingdom', *bemalkhut*, במלכות, has the same value.

[312] Here the general reference is to the fact that in this fourth layer of the soul words do not really exist. We are at the level of numbers, pure and simple. The specific reference is to the Tetragrammaton, also strongly embedded in the four, whose original pronunciation is unknown. This holiest of names was never pronounced except once a year on *Yom Kippur* by the high priest in the Holy of Holies. According to rabbinic tradition, once or twice in seven years the sages entrusted their disciples with the pronunciation of the Tetragrammaton. In all other cases this was forbidden.

³¹³ Reference to Ezekiel 34:25: 'And I will make with them a covenant of peace, and will cause the evil beasts to cease out of the land: and they shall dwell safely in the wilderness, and sleep in the woods.' 'In the wilderness' is *bamidbar*, במדבר, and amounts to 248, a number that will come up shortly. The horned woods refers to Daniel 7:7 where it states the following about the fourth beast: '..and it was diverse from all the beasts that were before it; and it had ten horns.' The ten horns are a reference to the ten *sefirot*.

³¹⁴ The four branches refer to the four rivers that branched off from the one flowing forth from the Garden of Eden (Gen. 2:10). They also denote the four letters of the Tetragrammaton, and its four spellings according to the four worlds. These four spellings together amount to 232. Reading the word *yiftach* (see endnote 310) as a directive to permute (in the sense of 'opening a word up' to find its additional meanings), and using the *abat* system to do so (because of the mention of 'his house' in Judges 11:34), the word following upon *yiftach*, *hamitspah*, המצפה, becomes 233. As well as spelling 'the tree of life', *ets ha-chayim*, עץ החיים, that is located in the Garden of Eden, this number contains the number 232 of the four spellings of the Tetragrammaton. In that capacity it now refers to the first four souls, which together with the last soul make for 233. The healing waters refer to Ezekiel 47:9: 'And it shall come to pass, that everything that lives, which moves, whithersoever the rivers shall come, shall live: and there shall be a very great multitude of fish, because these waters shall come thither: for they shall be healed; and everything shall live whither the river comes.' This verse contains the words 'living soul', *nefesh chayah* (see endnotes 7, 64, and 69). The immersion is a reference to the highly sanctified nature of the sphere the protagonist is now in.

³¹⁵ Reference to Ezekiel 34:25 (see endnote 313). The covenant implies the end of division, the end of understanding differences as opposites, the end,

in short, of discursive thought. At the level of the numbers, everything is abstract and objective.

[316] This turn-around refers to the last three letters of the fifteen foundation letters, which are reversed when compared to the order that instigated them: תום instead of מות (see endnote 301).

[317] Reference to the genesis of the *akhbal* system and the importance of Exodus 25:2 in it: 'Speak unto the children of Israel, that they bring me an offering: of every man that gives it willingly with his heart you shall take my offering.' See *To Kailash and Beyond*, chapter 8, *Where magic is rooted*.

318 Reference to Ezekiel 34:25 whose 'in the wilderness', *bamidbar*, במדבר, also amounts to 248 (see endnote 313). It also refers to the covenant (see endnote 315), *breit*, which after permutation with the *akhbal* system also acquires the number 248. The number 248 is furthermore the value of Abraham, אברהם, whose name refers to the *heh* with which the world was created: *beheh baram*, בהבראם (see Gen. 2:4). This *heh* points towards the five (souls, but also reference to the five times the word for death was used for this novel). Finally, according to Jewish tradition, a human is made up of 248 limbs.

[319] All parts of the protagonist are cut loose from their earthly bonds. The negational aspect of this occurrence is referred to by the use of 'free falling'. Womb is *rechem*, רחם, and amounts to 248 (see endnote 318). The womb of death refers to the fact that covenant, *breit*, through *akhbal* becomes 456. This number spells 'my death', *maveti*, מותי.

[320] Reference to Ezekiel 1:5: 'Also out of the midst thereof came the likeness of four living creatures. And this was their appearance; they had the likeness of a man.' This is the only appearance in Ezekiel of the plural form of 'beast', *chayah*: *chayot*. The reference here is to the five souls combined.

[321] The perspective is that of total mystical union with the godhead.

[322] All the opinionated thoughts and all the images ever made are now represented as the 'I' one has created. This 'I', having come to the realization that it is superfluous and harmful, by actually blocking out That-Which-Is, has come to negate itself. This is the gift that is being returned: the 'I' retreats in order for ultimate peace to exist. The reversal implied in this returning of the gift refers to the reversed order of the letters that make the word death at the end of the fifteen foundation letters (see endnote 301). Thoughts about negation are also amongst those returned: negation is negated.

BOOKS

O is a symbol of the world, of oneness and unity. In different cultures it also means the "eye," symbolizing knowledge and insight. We aim to publish books that are accessible, constructive and that challenge accepted opinion, both that of academia and the "moral majority."

Our books are available in all good English language bookstores worldwide. If you don't see the book on the shelves ask the bookstore to order it for you, quoting the ISBN number and title. Alternatively you can order online (all major online retail sites carry our titles) or contact the distributor in the relevant country, listed on the copyright page.

See our website **www.o-books.net** for a full list of over 500 titles, growing by 100 a year.

And tune in to myspiritradio.com for our book review radio show, hosted by June-Elleni Laine, where you can listen to the authors discussing their books.

MySpiritRadio